Everyday Islam

Religion and Tradition in Rural Central Asia

Sergei P. Poliakov

Edited with an Introduction by Martha Brill Olcott

Translated by Anthony Olcott

M.E. Sharpe
Armonk, New York
London, England

Copyright © 1992 by M. E. Sharpe, Inc.

All rights reserved. No part of this book may be reproduced in any form without written permission from the publisher, M. E. Sharpe, Inc. 80 Business Park Drive, Armonk, New York 10504.

Available in the United Kingdom and Europe from M. E. Sharpe, Publishers, 3 Henrietta Street, London WC2E 8LU.

Library of Congress Cataloging-in-Publication Data

Poliakov, Sergei Petrovich
[Bytovoi islam. English]
Everyday Islam : religion and tradition in Rural Central Asia
/ by Sergei P. Poliakov : edited with an introduction by
Martha Brill Olcott : translated by Anthony Olcott.
p. cm.
Translation of : Bytovoi islam.
Includes index.
ISBN 0-87332-673-3 (cloth)
ISBN 0-87332-674-1 (pbk.)
1. Soviet Central Asia—Politics and government.
2. Muslims—Soviet Central Asia.
3. Soviet Central Asia—Social life and customs.
4. Islam—Social aspects—Soviet Central Asia.
I. Olcott, Martha Brill, 1949–
II. Title.
DK859.P6513   1991
958′.400882971—dc20
91-20989
CIP
Photographs by the author.

Printed in the United States of America

The paper used in this publication meets the minimum requirements of American National Standard for Information Sciences— Permanence of Paper for Printed Library Materials, ANSI Z39.48–1984.

MV   10   9   8   7   6   5   4   3   2   1

CONTENTS

List of Tables and Figures	vii
Map of Central Asia	viii
Glossary	xi
By Way of Introduction *Martha Brill Olcott*	xiii

I. Background
1. Central Asian Traditionalism	3
2. Sources of Information	6
3. Some History	11

II. Economic Bases of Traditionalism
4. Traditionalism and the Economic Structure	23
5. Commercial Operations	32
6. Demographics and Employment	39
7. Private Enterprise and Livestock	46

III. Traditionalism and the Family
8. Central Asian Family Structure	53
9. Traditional Child Rearing	59
10. The Mahalla	76
11. Gender and Behavior	81
12. The Family Budget	87

IV. The Role of Religion in the Community
      13. Religious Institutions   95
      14. The Clergy   105

V. Social Dynamics of Traditionalism
      15. Traditionalism and the Working Class   115
      16. Traditionalism and the Intelligentsia   123
      17. Social Tensions   138

Notes   145

Index of Subjects   147

Index of Place Names   154

LIST OF TABLES AND FIGURES

Tables

1. Proportional Representation of the Peoples of Central Asia	8
2. Forms of Land Ownership and the Basic Structure of Power at the Mahalla Level of the Kishlak	14
3. Private Control of Land by Rural Residents	25
4. Distribution of Income and Expenditures of the Private Economy	36
5. Division of Income from Sale of Commodities at the Peasant Market	37
6. Transmission of Religious Information to Children	70
7. Sources of Information for Children in Rural Areas	73

Figures

1. Family Agricultural Economy	28
2. Transmission of Religious Information	68
3. The Rural Family Budget	88

Photos

Traditional Bride	64
Modern Bride	65
Fifteenth-Century Grave	102
Modern Grave of Party Functionary, Surrounded by Traditional Tombs	103

Central Asia

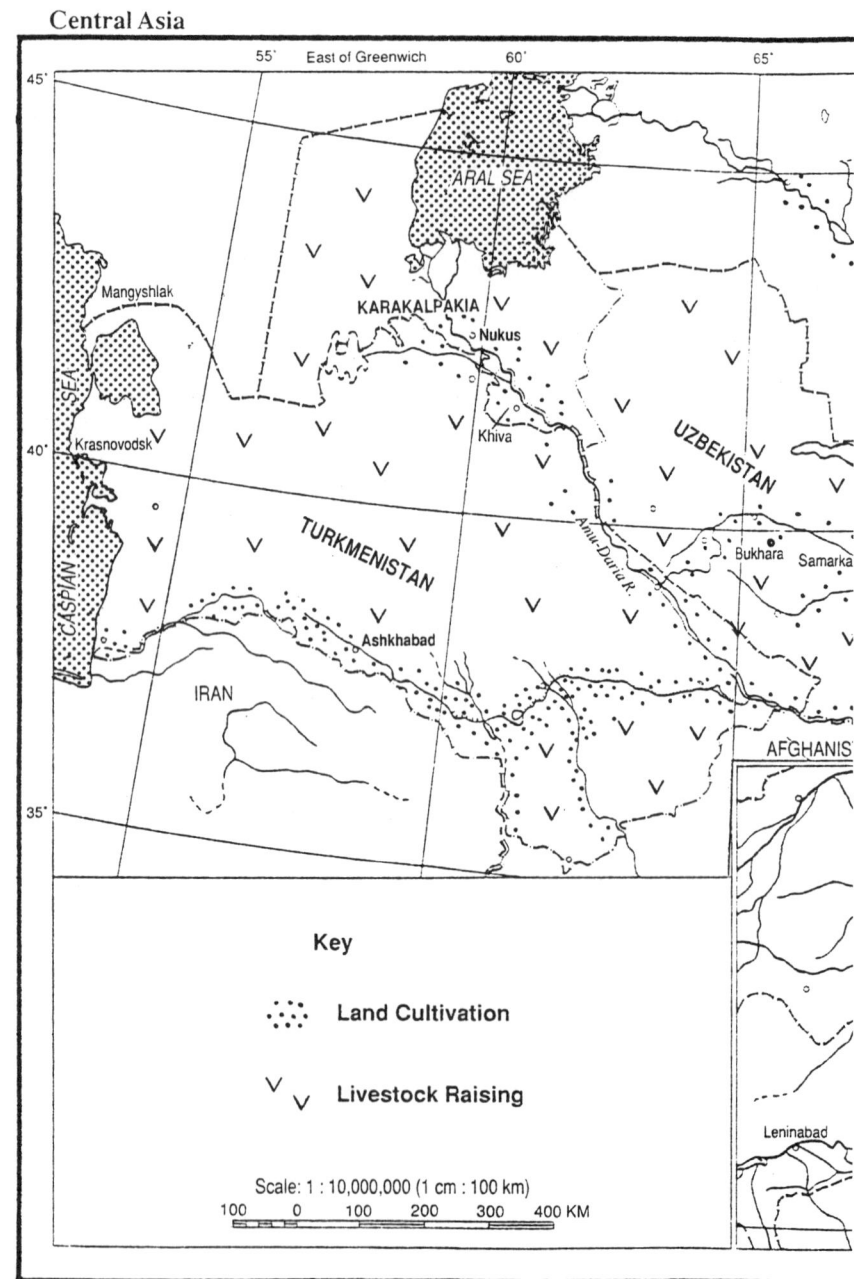

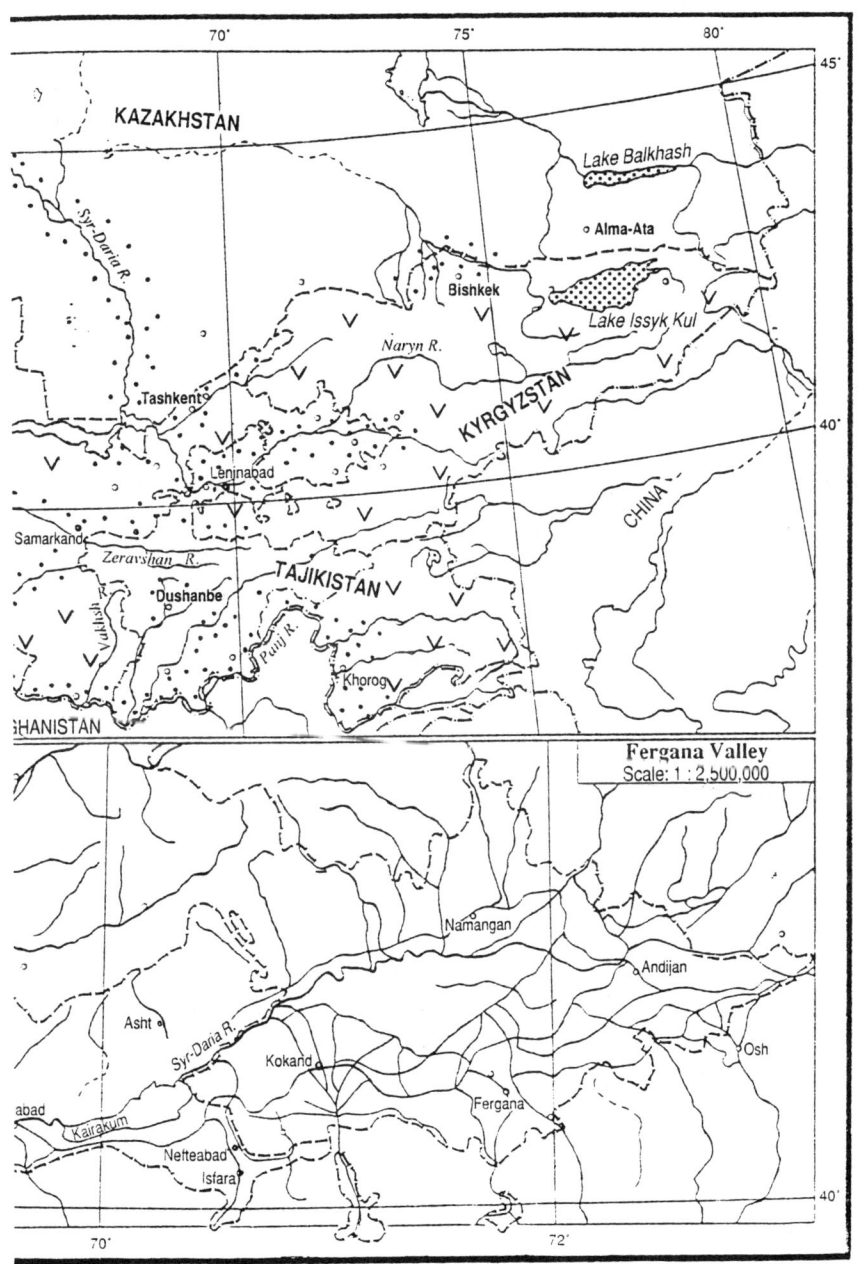

GLOSSARY

adat	(Turk.) customary or local traditional law
aksakal	(Turk.) village elder
aul	(Turk.) the residential unit of Kazakhs and Kirghiz; nomadic peoples organized their migrations by *aul*
avlod	(Taj.) a patrilineal clan
bibiotun	(Taj.) (Uzbek: ***otyncha***) woman who oversees observance of female ritual practices in a village
dekhan	(Pers.) peasant
hadith	(Arab.) the sayings of Mohammad
imam	(Arab.) prayer leader in a mosque
haj	(Arab.) pilgrimage to Mecca
kafir	(Arab.) infidel; one who is not a Muslim
kalym	(Turk.) bride-price paid by the groom's family
kishlak	(Turk.) village, originally a winter settlement
kolkhoz	(Russ. *kollektivnoe khoziaistvo*) collective farm. This form of collective ownership was introduced in Central Asia by the Soviet government between 1930 and 1938; the wages of collective-farm members (*kolkhozniki*) are based on the profitability of the farm
kurbash	(Turk.) leader
magi	(Arab.) ancient priestly class, supposed to have occult powers
mahalla	(Arab.) quarter, neighborhood, region
maktab	(Arab.) "underground" religious school
mazar	(Arab.) holy place (shrine), usually the grave of a "saint"
mullah	(Arab.) a Muslim cleric, a teacher of religious law
mullq	(Arab.) private property
oblast	(Rus.) province
raion	(Rus.) district

seid	(Arab.) honorofic for a descendant of Muhammad through the Prophet's grandson Hussein
shari'a	(Arab.) Islamic law
sheik	(Arab.) in Central Asia, the guardian of a mazar
sovkhoz	(Rus. *sovetskoe khoziaistvo*) state farm: a state-owned farm on which the farm workers (*sovkhozniki*) are paid a fixed wage
sunna	(Arab.) Islamic customs based on Mohammad's words and deeds
tura	(Mong.) descendants of Genghis Khan
ulema	(Arab.) Muslim theologians and scholars who interpret the Muslim legal system from a study of sources in the Koran and hadith
waqf	(Arab.) property belonging to a religious institution

BY WAY OF INTRODUCTION

The book you are about to read is likely to startle you and may even offend you, but it is certain to change your understanding of Central Asia. These were precisely the goals that Professor Sergei Petrovich Poliakov of Moscow State University—a Russian ethnographer in his mid-fifties and a lifelong member of the Communist party—set for himself in writing it. His aim was to produce a semischolarly account of the findings of more than thirty years of field research in Central Asia that would "stun" the reader into accepting his view of that world and the crisis that threatens it. For this reason I decided not to edit the manuscript to make it conform to American academic norms. Sergei Petrovich is going to speak to you in his own words and describe reality as he sees it. My purpose here is simply to introduce you to both the author and his subject.

The book falls into the genre of what in Russian is called *publitsistika*. It is a journalistic work insofar as the author is trying to shape opinion, but it is not a work of "communist propaganda." Sergei Petrovich genuinely holds the views he sets forth here. Indeed, this is the first work Poliakov has written that he feels reflects his honest and freely given opinion, for the book is wholly uncensored.

Poliakov feels some urgency to convey his views, for he believes that a deepening demographic crisis in Central Asia indicates a need for fundamental change. He believes Central Asia to be mired down by the weight of traditionalism—that is, by "everyday Islam": the customs, values, and economic practices of traditional rural Islamic society. In Poliakov's view these age-old folkways, reinforced by religious authority and traditional elites, are at the root of the region's stagnation; only by breaking with that past can Central Asia become a modern and prosperous society.

Central Asians themselves now blame their plight on seventy-odd years of Soviet rule and the decades of Russian tsarist colonial rule that preceded it. Although he recognizes and acknowledges these sentiments, it is Poliakov's view that traditional Central Asian elites were able to suborn and subordinate the Communist party in their region long ago, so that they are fully responsible for current ills. Poliakov's position is at odds with traditional Soviet historiography, which maintained that the Central Asian masses welcomed Soviet rule (and sometimes even tsarist rule) as a liberation from a benighted past. It is also in conflict with the recent revisionist historiography of the academic establishment in Central Asia, which has undertaken a more "even-handed" treatment of the region's resistance to Russian domination.

A further reason for Poliakov's sense of urgency is his belief that Soviet policy decisions in recent years served only to exacerbate the problems of Central Asia. He is critical of the Gorbachev regime and what he sees as the deepening political entrenchment and expanding economic power of the region's traditional elites. Poliakov does not criticize the principles of decentralization or republic sovereignty *per se*. He believes, however, that the decisions of the past several years have not empowered the people of Central Asia but rather have given traditional elites vast new resources to use to exploit the region's masses.

Like Poliakov, many Central Asian political reformers would criticize the way the policies of *perestroika* have been applied in their region. At the same time, however, they would certainly reject his vision of what the future of Central Asia should be. Poliakov is a strong advocate of the idea of "modernity." He believes that society is intended to be constructed on scientific principles and that if it is so constituted, all citizens will benefit.

In his view, all societies must become urbanized and industrialized, with men and women integrated into the economy on a roughly equal basis.

Poliakov scorns the proposition that an Islamic society is a just society constructed according to the dictates of the "true faith." As he sees it, religion has been used as a tool of control and a means of denying people their economic and political rights in Central Asia. Though not himself a religious believer, Poliakov is respectful toward those who are, providing they share his commitment to modernity and do not "obstruct" the "scientific" grounding of the social order. He is a strong proponent of the idea that a society must be rooted in universally held moral principles; he believes that fully secular and even atheistic societies are capable of being so constructed.

As a materialist, Poliakov believes that economic relationships dictate or shape politics. He also believes that the working out of "economic laws" takes on a unique form in Islamic societies, where religion, culture, politics, and economics are so closely intertwined. Thus, for example, he rejects the contention of an earlier generation of Soviet scholars that politics in Central Asia was shaped by its "feudal" nature. In Poliakov's view Central Asia never went through a feudal period, for the conditions of economic development there did not mirror those of Europe.

At the same time, Poliakov also rejects the premise of Muslim believers that there is such a thing as a uniquely Islamic society and that Central Asia's Islamic heritage has "preordained" a particular economic system or eternal political domination by a particular social stratum—those who can claim privileged descent from Muhammad or a priestly caste.

Although it is not always apparent, Islam as a religious faith is not the object of attack in this book. Poliakov's target is "traditionalism"—in his terms, a particular form of economic and social control that is legitimated by religion. He believes that the traditional elite has misconstrued and manipulated Islam in order to keep the Central Asian masses under its domination. Poliakov does not directly assert that they do so venally; he is willing to accept a more culturally specific explanation than a classical Marxist might advance. Because Central Asia has had relatively restricted contact with the wider world, including the Islamic world, he believes, Islam is easily invoked and interpreted in a way that will suit the needs of those in control of the society.

One of the interesting features of Poliakov's study is the case he makes for the *continuity* of social order in Central Asia despite decades of Soviet rule. He argues that the traditional elites of Central Asia were able to reestablish themselves after the Bolshevik revolution and their seeming defeat in the 1920s and 1930s. He considers it one of the best-kept secrets of Central Asia that prerevolutionary social position is still the most important determinant of social position today.

As a communist, Poliakov is angered by the way traditional Central Asian elites have used the Soviet state structure and the Communist party organization to retain their hold on society, particularly in the post-Stalin period. During these years the leading families of the region, supposedly destroyed during the period of civil war, used their secondary and tertiary branches to penetrate the Communist party. By the 1960s their members were assuming positions of control in their republics, and by the 1970s and early 1980s they were fully in command of the regional economy.

Poliakov is a strong defender of the two Moscow procurators—Teleman Gdlian and Nikolai Ivanov—who were sent to Uzbekistan in the mid-1980s to "clean up" the local Communist party and the cotton industry with it. Gdlian and Ivanov uncovered a scheme that involved the theft of millions of rubles annually from state funds. Implicated in the scandal were the party leadership of several oblasts, the republic government of Uzbekistan, and possibly even members of the Politburo in Moscow. When the investigation cast a shadow on Egor Ligachev in 1989, Gdlian and Ivanov were themselves dismissed for "excesses."

Poliakov considers this story illustrative of the way in which the Central Asian traditional economy has evaded the best efforts of the planners in Moscow. The organs of Soviet power have been used by the traditional elite, backed by religious authority, to foster the second economy and to extract part of the "surplus" the second economy produces to perpetuate their control. In Poliakov's opinion, this "second," underground economy, now being "legalized" through the introduction of property rights, has bled the population of its potential for economic growth. He implicitly believes that only through collective or communal ownership can majority rights be protected from minority exploitation. Private ownership can safely be introduced, in Poliakov's view, only when the system it replaces has been based on egalitarian values; otherwise, private ownership will only deepen mass exploitation. Central Asia is not an egalitarian society today, he believes, precisely because collective ownership was never fully established in the region and the traditional elite never lost economic dominance.

Poliakov believes that the existing fusion of tradition and the Soviet system, and the pervasiveness of the traditional power structure, has been the source of political stability in Central Asia. In his view, the innovations of the Gorbachev era actually worsened the prospects for fundamental change in Central Asia by creating new levers for the traditional elite to manipulate. He fears, for example, that land reform will further institutionalize the existing economic power relationships and that the new legislatures will be used to ratify this as an expression of "democratic" will. He fears that Islam, now being elevated to something approaching a state religion—and indeed, Islamic clerics are becoming active in legislative politics—will be used to bind Central Asian society to the system even more tightly.

Poliakov's purpose in writing this book was to shed light on what he views as a preventable crisis-in-the-making in Central Asia; it was not to "name names" or document malfeasance. One of the reasons Poliakov did not choose the documentary approach was that it might compromise the many Central Asian students and friends who have explained their society and opened their homes to him over decades of research in the field.

xviii   INTRODUCTION

Poliakov does have a great deal of information to support many of his conclusions, however. As I worked with him on the manuscript he generously offered me dozens of hours for discussion about this study and about Central Asian politics more generally. In addition, he gave me virtually unrestricted access to his library, including his manuscript and slide collections. I also met extensively with several of his former students, now well-respected scholars in Moscow and in their home republics in Central Asia. Through these hours of conversation, and the access to his own field work and that of his students that Poliakov has afforded me, I have gained a deep respect for the man, for the depth of his knowledge, and for the quality of his work. Yet at the same time, I could not but observe that Sergei Petrovich is as much shaped by his heritage as he perceives the Central Asians to be.

Poliakov is the product of a Soviet intellectual upbringing. He is an economic determinist who believes that a society that has an egalitarian economic system will inevitably develop a "just" social structure as well. Thus he is confident that if thoroughgoing economic reform were introduced in Central Asia, the region's social problems would begin to be rectified.

For Poliakov it is unthinkable that a population could of its own "free will" decide to give cultural preservation priority over economic development. He is simply unable to accept the proposition. He believes that societies that defend the primacy of religion do so because those in control have undertaken to "blind" the masses to their own interests. In Poliakov's view, no rational being would ever sacrifice his economic self-interest once it was explained to him in terms he could understand.

Poliakov is a convinced believer in social science, in the premise that society can be studied "scientifically." He believes, moreover, that the application of scientific methods to social observation offers a real potential for healing. From this flows his belief that Central Asia's problems could be "cured" if it were subjected to a "scientifically" constructed economic policy.

Throughout his text Poliakov looks to "science" to "prove" his points. Hence he makes extensive use of charts and diagrams to illuminate the nature of social relationships. Sometimes his criteria for quantification and empirical "proof" are simply inexplicable. In fact, we spent several hours arguing over whether to retain the charts that he prepared for the original manuscript. In the end I decided to submit to his judgment, though not because I think this material will contribute much to the reader's understanding of Central Asian society. What the charts do best is illuminate the existing state of Soviet ethnographic analysis as it is taught to the talented undergraduate and graduate students at Moscow State University.

These caveats aside, there is a great wealth of information in this book that is made accessible to readers of English for the first time. One of the highlights of the work is Poliakov's discussion of the demographic situation in Central Asia. The region has one of the world's highest birthrates and a declining standard of living—ingredients for social disaster. This, in Poliakov's opinion, is Central Asia's major problem, and he believes that the policies of the Gorbachev years have only deepened the emergency.

Poliakov's understanding of this crisis is rather different from that of most Western analysts. Like them, Poliakov sees the population increase as a manifestation of the Islamic character of Central Asian society. But while Western experts often interpret the population increase as a conscious or unconscious religio-political expression, Poliakov sees the genesis of the problem in purely economic terms.

The population increase is being fueled, in his opinion, by the labor-intensive nature of the region's second, traditional economy. Central Asians need to have large families to keep this economy functioning smoothly, and this in turn puts unacceptable strains on the population and on the natural resources of the region.

The book offers detailed and hitherto unavailable descriptions of the operations of the second economy, including the ways in which business is transacted, profit is realized, and capital is secured. Through this account, the reader gets some sense of the scope of this economy and the scale of trade that it has long operated outside of official control. In Poliakov's opinion, the second economy has completely usurped the primacy of the state economy in Central Asia, as people give the greater part of their time and attention, and even priority in the use of state-owned equipment, to work on privately held lands. This information sheds new light on the likely paths for a transition from "communism" in the region.

Poliakov ties all of the basic features of "everyday" rural life in Central Asia to the second economy, and he provides a rich and detailed description of that culture. His discussion of family life and the interweaving of family roles with the division of labor in the rural community is far more comprehensive than earlier accounts. He shows how little family life has changed in most rural areas of Central Asia. He bolsters his case for the interdependence of economics and traditional life by providing data from some industrialized pockets in rural Central Asia where traditional cultural norms have begun to break down.

Poliakov also offers richly detailed descriptions of female society, which, because of its almost complete segregation from male society, has been closed not only to Western scholars but to male Soviet investigators as well. Poliakov's research team has always included female students and scholars drawn from the very communities that he is studying, and his wife always travels with the expedition as a chaperone for the unmarried women in the group.

As the female team members have always been required to observe the same social mores as the local women, Poliakov's expeditions have had far greater success with participant observation than other Soviet teams. He is able to describe in detail the continued vitality of customary marital practices that other Soviet scholars until recently maintained were long dead, such as the payment of a *kalym* (bride price), polygamy, child marriage, and the kidnapping of women.

Poliakov is personally disturbed by what he considers to be the desperate plight of rural Central Asian women. Women in the traditional community virtually always have their lives planned out from birth, fully geared toward the fulfillment of their roles as wives and mothers. They progress from being mothers-in-training to being young brides, then mothers, and eventually—if they are lucky and bear sons—mothers-in-law and heads of households. He also describes the fate of those women who, whether by nature, by inadvertence, or by volition, fail to fulfill these roles. Here the reader is given valuable insights into the phenomenon of female suicide in Central Asia.

While Poliakov's judgmental tone may seem strident at times, it is hard not to be troubled by these descriptions of the life that rural Central Asian women endure. In fact, their hardships are arguably even more severe than what Poliakov details, as he omits discussion of the poor medical care available to pregnant women and newborn babies, and the long-term health hazards posed by frequent childbearing, poor diet, and environmental conditions in Central Asia.

The book also offers a hitherto unavailable glimpse into the operation of male society through Poliakov's discussion of the *mahalla*. These neighborhood organizations are characteristic of urban as well as rural communities, but in rural areas, where their roles overlap with the religious and economic spheres of the community, they are undoubtedly the principal regulators of social behavior. The officials of the mahalla serve as intermediaries regulating the taxation of the second economy and the community's disbursement of funds to local religious organizations. Significantly, the mahalla committee traditionally chooses the members of the local soviet.

The mahalla, of course, can only regulate the behavior of individuals who fall within its jurisdiction, those who reside in the traditional community or live among relatives—as many young male workers do not. Poliakov argues that traditional Central Asian society has a tendency to infantilize males (in rural areas they often do not head their own households until they are forty years old). These two factors, Poliakov hypothesizes, explain the wildly destructive behavior that in recent years has turned mass protests into riots in the large cities of the region. It is, in fact, generally accepted that the majority of rioters have been rural youths living away from home, but most Central Asian observers would certainly object to this as a sufficient explanation of the disturbances that have occurred in Fergana, Alma-Ata, and Dushanbe.

My own observations, which have been restricted to urban communities, bear out Poliakov's conclusion that the mahalla is the center of effective local power in all but the most newly settled regions of Central Asia. (The only other exceptions would be in traditionally nomadic populations, where kinship rather than community groups predominate.) It seems beyond doubt that the mahalla will grow in influence as the power of the Communist party wanes.

The other institution that is sure to gain as party authority declines is organized religion. Poliakov's discussion of the role of religion in rural Central Asia may well be the most valuable part of his book. His descriptions of the pervasiveness of religion, the existence of a widespread network of religious schools, the ability of Islamic authorities to tax the population systematically, and the religious observances of women will be entirely new for most Western readers.

After this book was written, the laws governing the relations between church and state in the Soviet Union were liberalized. The "unofficial," underground religious establishment that has long dominated rural Central Asia was "legalized." However, if the conclusions of Poliakov's most recent research are accurate, the unofficial clergy is still locked in conflict with the officially recognized, formal religious establishment—namely, SADUM, the Spiritual Administration of Central Asia and Kazakhstan. Since the late 1980s SADUM has been able to open mosques in every major community in the region. In many cases, however, what this has really meant is official recognition of already existing but unsanctioned mosques and religious schools staffed by unofficial clerics.

Although many of the unofficial clerics had previously maintained informal contacts with SADUM, they were independent of its authority since they had not risen through the ranks of the formal religious establishment. They were therefore considered "unstable." The unofficial clerics tended in turn to be distrustful of SADUM because of what they saw as its cooptation by the state. In Poliakov's opinion the alliance of the unofficial clerics with SADUM is a temporary one, and SADUM will try to replace them as quickly as it is able to get new clergy through its newly established seminaries in the region or through SADUM-sponsored foreign training.

The authority of the official religious establishment, however, has been compromised by close association with the Communist party. Further complicating the situation is the fact that SADUM—based in Tashkent, the capital of Uzbekistan—has already been weakened as an institution by the efforts of the party leaderships in other republics to set up their own religious establishments.

These efforts are being undertaken with the intention of conferring greater legitimacy on local party elites, enabling them to protect their own power bases from the party's decay. Over the past few years Central Asian party officials have fully reversed their official stand on religion. Previously they hid whatever observance of religious rituals they engaged in, but now it is politically expedient to demonstrate respect for Islam. Today they attend religious ceremonies and even make a show of observing Islamic customs such as publicly reciting a prayer after eating.

The efforts of republic officials to cultivate new religious establishments have an economic angle as well. For example, the Communist party of Kyrgyzstan (Kirgizia), headed by the deposed president of the republic, Absamat Masaliev, decided to hand over the twelve-story marble building that was Central Committee headquarters to a newly established "independent" Muslim center. This occurred, coincidentally, shortly after Saudi Arabia had agreed to make substantial lines of credit available to Kazakhstan. It seemed obvious that Masaliev hoped to enlist the support of not only Allah but also Saudi Arabia in the cause of his own political comeback.

While politics on this level is outside the purview of Poliakov's study, his detailed analysis of the ways in which religion is integrated with traditional rural life gives grounds for doubt that any strategy for severing the two could succeed. If Poliakov is correct, it is traditional rural society that will "restructure" the official religious establishment, and not the other way around; nor will the efforts of party officials to derive legitimacy from official religious institutions prove successful in the long term.

Poliakov's concluding discussions on social groups and social tensions make clear how skeptical he is that Central Asian elites will be able to cope adequately with the crises their society must confront. Readers who object to the harsh tenor of Poliakov's judgments or the substance of his alternative should not be as quick to dismiss his conclusion. The point that Poliakov is making is an important one and, upon reflection, a difficult one to reject.

Poliakov is convinced that the thrust of politics in Soviet Central Asia today is backward-looking—essentially an effort to undo more than a century of Russian domination. This, he believes, is the impetus for the current glorification of Islam and of a "pure," pre-Soviet and pre-Russian, Central Asian past. But Poliakov, well-versed in Central Asian history, finds in it no idyll to recover; indeed, he finds reason to believe that the past was a good deal harsher than the present.

For all his ideological preconceptions, Poliakov is a pragmatist, able to separate his own communist utopian sentiments from an assessment of real conditions (and he would be among the first to admit that the Communist regime has not lived up to its own precepts). Thus he is alarmed by the proclivity of many Central Asian intellectuals to idealize their past and fantasize about their future. Most Western scholars who have spent time in Central Asia will have noticed this trend among at least some of the intellectuals who are attempting to organize the political opposition in the region today.

When one gets the opportunity to interview widely among the various levels of the Central Asian elite, it is hard to shake the impression that, over all, "the best and the brightest" are to be found in the party elite. These people clearly command the intelligence, political skill, and administrative experience that they will need to ride out the transition from the Soviet system. But Poliakov is skeptical that even the younger generation of the elite will use their power properly—to benefit the masses. In his view their cultural blinders render them incapable of perceiving the solutions to the crises their region must confront.

Of course, the new generation that is beginning to assume positions of authority and responsibility in Central Asia has one advantage that its elders lacked: greatly expanded exposure to conditions outside the region and outside the USSR, both in the Muslim world and in the West. But even here, Poliakov finds alarming tendencies. As he points out, the trend in education is away from instruction in Russian (long mandated as the language of "interethnic communication" in the USSR) in favor of native-language education and the introduction of study of Arabic as a foreign language. This is disturbing to Poliakov, a champion of modernization and the study of "world" languages, by which he means Russian and Western languages. In his view, this trend in education signals that national cultural concerns have been given priority over the necessity for rapid economic development, thus jeopardizing the very survival of the society itself.

In sum, Poliakov believes that the current political leadership of Central Asia is moving in the wrong direction. He doubts that the region will be able to absorb its rapid population growth without a major industrialization effort. But the way that property is currently being divided will, he believes, further reduce the incentives for Central Asians to leave the countryside. He is concerned, moreover, that the spread of family farms will make impossible the type of large-scale farming that is required if the region is to develop a subsistence economy and to feed its population. In Poliakov's view, by adopting policies that both benefit themselves and win popularity, rather than policies of rapid modernization, the political leadership of Central Asia is speeding the region toward disaster. And yet he believes, just as assuredly, that their political power remains secure.

Notwithstanding my unwillingness to join in Poliakov's caustic critique of Islamic traditionalism, I find many of his conclusions compelling. The more I travel through Central Asia, the easier I find it to accept Poliakov's basic premise that the traditional society has been modified but not essentially disrupted by the colonial experience. I share his view that Islamic traditions will be the wellspring of the region's political and cultural future, although, unlike Poliakov, I do not believe that this need be negative. That will depend on the skill, and luck, of the Central Asians themselves. And it is they, after all, who should have the responsibility for finally coming to terms with their own past and making the decisions that will shape their future. One can only hope, for their own sake, that their sense of grievance will not lead them to make decisions that are ill-considered.

Poliakov is not dispassionate. His outlook is shaped not only by his own cultural assumptions and ideological preconceptions—just as the reader's will be—but also by his love of Central Asia and its people, and a desire to appreciate their past, understand their present, and improve their future. I am persuaded that we can learn something from him.

Martha Brill Olcott
Colgate University

I

BACKGROUND

1

Central Asian Traditionalism

> *They ask thee what they should spend in charity. Say: Whatever ye spend that is good, is for parents and kindred and orphans and those in want and for wayfarers.*   The Koran, II, 215
>
> *And lo, in reward God sent me disillusionment.*   Rudaki

This work is the first attempt to understand the enormously complex and contradictory phenomenon of traditionalism as it exists in the Soviet republics of Central Asia. What is traditionalism?

Over many years of studying the traditional economy and way of life of the population of the Central Asian republics, we have asked thousands of respondents the same two questions: "How do you live, following what norms? What defines your way of life?" There were no other questions in this questionnaire, and the forms distinguished only the sex and age of the respondent. Three-quarters of the respondents were male, one-quarter were female. The most complete answers were given by people of middle age and older, while answers by younger people, especially by young women, were only rarely complete. But with very few exceptions the answer to the first question was always the same: "We live as our fathers devised," "We live as Muslims." The second part of the question got only one answer: "Tradition."

This term is often used in studies, but not all authors who write about the phenomenon assign it the same meaning. Without entering into a polemic, I would note that in this work the terms "tradition" and "traditionalism" are fairly broadly understood and are applied only to Central Asia. This is not traditionalist Islam, meaning the various intellectual currents that preach a return to an earlier Islamic society. When designating a society based strictly upon Koranic practices I prefer the term Wahhabism. I know of no groups or ideological currents in Central Asia that would completely and utterly support a society that professes as its main human values those laid out in the Koran and that follows the Koran in everyday life. Declarations to that effect are not supported by practice.

I use "traditionalism" and "traditional society" to mean the complete rejection of anything new introduced from the outside into the familiar, "traditional" way of life. Traditionalism does not simply battle novelty; it actively demands constant correction of the life-style according to an ancient, primordial, or "classical" model. It makes no difference to traditionalism what that model springs from, whether it is of Islamic, Christian, or some other origin. The only thing that is important is that society must not depart from its "ideal form."

This form is defended from the world outside by an ideological superstructure whose fundamental ideas control the masses of the population and so become a material force. It is the superstructure that guarantees the most favorable conditions for the operation of the economic base that formed it. This superstructure cannot exist outside the given economic system, and its well-being depends directly upon the flourishing of the base.

In all traditional societies the superstructure is given very great attention, first of all because the superstructure influences the system of intergenerational transmission of information. The younger generation receives only that information which promotes preservation of the traditional way of life. Any other information is omitted. This purposeful selection is manifested in everything—economic life, ideology (including religious ideology), cultural values, attitudes toward the environment, and so on. At the same time it is important to remember that the transformation of a traditionalist society can proceed only by traditional methods. An example of this is the problem of regulating family size, as solved by the *ulema* of Al-Azhar in Cairo.

I have not made it my goal to describe all aspects of the manifestation of traditionalism with the same degree of thoroughness. A proper examination of traditionalism would require a series of independent studies of the various aspects of that way of life. The first steps in that direction have already been taken: the system of traditional education of children in rural Uzbek families, the traditional types of economy among the foothill Kirgiz and Tajiks, and the history of the formation of settlements in northern Tajikistan have already been studied. For this last territory there have also been studies of the rural mosques and other religious structures. A study of the "heritage" of the ancient religious systems that existed on the territory of Central Asia is in the process of completion. However, studies of this sort should be under way continuously, taking account of all the changes occurring in our society. Only then might scholarship influence everyday practice.[1]

I make no effort to join in attempts to criticize traditionalism as a system, attempts that I consider extremely unsuccessful. The common practice of criticizing a way of life without discovering the social and economic bases on which it exists in our society is pointless. My basic stress is not on criticism of life values but on explanation of the persistence and "dynamism" of traditionalism as a way of life among a part of our country's population. Criticizing a situation without offering an alternative is simply carping. As for alternatives, their argumentation, elaboration, and detailed explanation would demand more than one book. The complexity of such a study is so great that it would not permit omission of any material that might demonstrate the relevance of actions.

The present work introduces value judgments only in the case of phenomena that demand society's immediate response.

2

Sources of Information

The present work draws on the data accumulated over a thirty-year period by the Central Asian Expedition of the History Faculty of Moscow State University. The main task of this expedition is the study of the historical ethnography of Central Asia. The chronological frame of study is the second millennium of this era, although certain problems require going further back, to the middle of the first millennium.

Depending upon the specific scientific requirements of study in one period or another, the expedition is made up of archaeologists, anthropologists, and ethnographers. The collection of material follows a unified program, which allows comparison at all levels; the tasks for each team contain the same major categories, the details reflecting the specifics of the given discipline. For example, each program includes a section that asks: "What are the origins of this regional group of the population?" Each of the three disciplines answers the question in its own way. All three teams must study the region that this group of people occupies. One result of this method is that the data obtained are comparable.

The areas that have been studied are the northern, western, and southern regions of Turkmenistan; the Samarkand, Bukhara, and Kashkadaria oblasts and the Fergana valley in Uzbekistan; Mangyshlak Oblast and the area around Lake Balkhash in Kazakhstan; the northern and western regions of Kyrgyzstan; and all of Tajikistan, except for the Pamirs. The information that is collected is not subject to analysis by the government. The data reflect various aspects of daily life among the Central Asian population, primarily the rural population—for example, their religious beliefs and their use of the water resources and geographical zones that are outside of state control. Included is objective demographic information about the economic activity of the family and the social structure and ethnic situation at the village level. Written sources and archaeological materials are used to study the medieval history of Central Asia, so that the various aspects of life in Central Asian society become part of a dynamic. Processes arising in the Middle Ages and those arising in more modern times, including the present, are studied separately and are compared.

A special methodology, based on statistical techniques, has been elaborated to extract information from nonquantitative field materials and to translate results into numerical expression. This methodology permits the resolution of a whole range of problems, because it makes apparent the hidden processes that are inaccessible to traditional descriptive methodologies. The distinguishing factor in this methodology, unlike the majority of modern methodologies, is that we do not draw our conclusions based on the number of people surveyed or from the number of monuments from material culture studied. This does not mean that quantitative representation is not important; during our work we surveyed thousands of informants. What is important is that we were interested not in establishing people's opinions about events, but rather in establishing historical fact. Once a fact is established, then a system for verifying that fact is elaborated. The main advantage of the methodology is that theoretical computations are easily tested in practice by using census materials and by forecasting the location of archaeological monuments and the dynamics of various aspects of the life of society. "The viewpoint of life and practice must be the first and basic viewpoint for a theory of knowledge," V.I. Lenin wrote.[2] An example of this process of verification is the proportional relationship of various nationalities found in the materials from the expedition, as tested against materials drawn from other sources.

Verifying materials exist for four of the five historical and

Table 1

Proportional Representation of the Peoples of Central Asia (%)

Ethnic group	Field materials	1926 Census
Tajik	24	17.26
Uzbek	64	69.26
Turkmen	12	13.48

cultural zones of Central Asia that have mixed population (Khorezm, northern Tajikistan, Samarkand and environs, southern Tajikistan, and the Fergana valley). For Khorezm, Samarkand, and northern and southern Tajikistan, the results achieved using field materials to fix the proportional constituency of the ethnic composition of these areas are identical to those given by the census data and archival materials for the end of the nineteenth century and the first quarter of the twentieth. Study of the proportional representation of peoples in the population of *part* of Central Asia, based on field materials, gives results identical to the *overall* relationship of Tajiks, Uzbeks, and Turkmens according to the 1926 census. The materials of the expedition show the same tempo of population growth for the past fifty years as does the all-union census; the Uzbeks, for example, have increased by 2.5 percent per year.

Use of this methodology reduces the area over which archaeological monuments must be searched for significantly. For example, after comparing the indicators for medieval Zoroastrianism in the regions of Central Asia studied, we established that the greatest likelihood of finding such monuments was in Leninabad Oblast of Tajikistan, where a search was undertaken, and a large group of archaeological sites was discovered. These attested to the presence of a Zoroastrian religious center there up until the eighth century A.D.

Finally, this methodology has made clear that in modern times traditionalism has become more active in the cattle-breeding regions of Central Asia, such as in northwestern Turkmenistan (part of contemporary Krasnovodsk Oblast). Sociological studies of religiosity conducted among the population of the oblast in

1984 confirmed this conclusion. The events in Alma-Ata in December 1986 also attest to the growth of traditionalism.* Another example is an especially noticeable upsurge of ritual practice in Mangyshlak, to be seen primarily in the widely distributed building of burial mausoleums (costing up to twenty thousand rubles) and the construction of mosques on the sites of medieval burial grounds. Particularly common is the use, as mosques, of wholly or partially underground funeral vaults constructed in antiquity by the Saks.† Islamic festivals are actively celebrated, whereas twenty-five years ago nothing of the sort occurred.

These detailed examples of how the results received are checked are necessary to confirm the reliability of conclusions drawn. Unfortunately, the study of contemporary traditionalism does not always convey an accurate picture, for reasons that are complex and often unclear. The great majority of [Soviet] studies use unacceptable methodological bases for understanding the phenomenon of traditionalism, which is understood and evaluated solely as the residue of early forms of civic consciousness. In part this is due to the incompleteness, or more often simple unsuitability, of the way in which primary information is collected (through questionnaires). These studies lead to a false picture, at all levels, of the real significance of traditionalism in Central Asian society.

Traditionalism has never been just a holdover, in the Marxist meaning of the term, since Central Asian society has always contained groups that strive to preserve old ways and regard the past as having been a "golden age" for them. Traditionalism has always been a reflection of the social and economic structure, a way of life based on a specific economic structure[3]—a combination of cultivation of irrigated land and extensive livestock breeding, with a very large role played by secondary trade. This is precisely how Russian scholars understood traditionalism; details of this approach may be found, for example, in the works of Academi-

---

*See page 81, below.
†This is the general name for the primarily steppe population of Central Asia in the first centuries of the current era.

cian V.V. Barthold,[4] the great nineteenth-century Russian orientalist. Researchers' departure from such an understanding must be regarded as a bad mistake that has led to negative consequences in practical applications both inside and outside our country.

In this connection it is impossible to agree with those who regard traditionalism within the USSR as distinct from the same phenomenon outside of our country. This view has not been mandated anywhere and is not written down, but it does exist within the Soviet scholarly community. This approach to studying traditionalism is particularly apparent in the studies of contemporary Islamic society which in essence proclaim the existence of a special "Soviet" Islam radically different from its "aggressive" foreign cousin. This bias (deliberate or inadvertent) in the practical study of contemporary religiosity in Central Asia, combined with a theoretical claim of the "peculiarity" of Islam in the USSR, has created an utterly false picture of the "safety" of Islam in the USSR and of its "dying-out" in our country. The idea that religion is dying out has been declaimed very actively in our country, based on the growth of mass consciousness, which signifies the victory of the materialist world view. However, at the same time, the fact that materialism is the world view of the industrial proletariat, and not of the petit-bourgeois peasant class, has been actively silenced. It is precisely this latter class that predominates in Central Asia. Even now social stratification is far from optimal for the dissemination of materialism. The infrequent admissions that have recently appeared in the press about the attraction Islam holds for "a few young people" are not to be taken seriously. Improving the existing situation demands not only the radical reexamination of the theoretical aspects of the problem, but also a different method of organizing and collecting primary information in the field. This last circumstance also makes the question of how ethnographers are trained an urgent one. Only an ethnographic approach to the study of actual practices can provide a true picture of the condition of society. Practice has shown that other approaches provide false information, which leads to unreliable conclusions.

3

Some History

> *Lo! Abraham said to his father Azar: Takest thou idols for gods?*
> The Koran, VI, 74

Usually traditionalism is seen as some sort of unit, in both form and content, to be discovered only by studying rituals, dwellings, clothing, and so forth. Religious beliefs and ideas are examined more fully, at the highest plane of analysis. The philosophical aspect of Islam, for example, is studied on a high theological plane, political structure is studied on the level of the Islamic state, and so forth. Life in the villages is examined from the same heights, putting the Islamic world view of the ulema on the same level as that of illiterate peasants. The same reductive approach is also characteristic for studying forms of property and other legal norms.

The analysis of the economic structures of Asian society in the great majority of studies is simply incorrect. The invention of "Asiatic feudalism" as a full analogue of European feudal society was a logical conclusion to the creation of an unreal picture of Asian society at all levels of its existence.* Asian medieval society is fundamentally distinguished from European feudal society by the fact that in Asian society the primary producer was always free and was not forcibly bound to the land. Land itself was

---

*What Poliakov is developing here is a critique of the Soviet practice of dividing all history into prehistoric, feudal, capitalist, and socialist epochs, in strict application of Marxist maxims.

under the control of the peasant, and so was his property. Moreover, this could be not only personal property, but also collective or communal ownership of land. Land could be sold, or freely alienated. Further, the periodization of the social and political history of mankind that Karl Marx proposed arbitrarily omitted the Asiatic mode of production.

This has led to important errors. For example, disregard for the indivisibility of religious and civil authority in the Islamic world (at least before the second half of the twentieth century) has led to Islam's being understood only as a religion. The majority of researchers simply do not consider it necessary to note that Islam as a religion does not have its own church organization, and that in Islamic society, state organs are at the same time religious. Yet, it is precisely this structure that guarantees the tenacity of Islamic society in the modern world. If there exists a "religious" Islamic institution, a mosque, then that means, in the conditions of modern Central Asia, that there also exists a local, fundamental "state" Islamic nucleus of society—the village, or *kishlak* (in rural areas), or the urban neighborhood organization called the *mahalla* (which also exists in rural settlements). Concrete examples and details of this situation will be given below.

Understanding Islam only as a religion also allowed comparison (on structural levels) of *shari'a*, or Islamic law, with Roman law, while forgetting that Roman law was never Christian church law. It must not be forgotten that the Koran, unlike the Bible, regulates the Muslim's entire life and defines the forms of property and the state structure of Muslim society.

One very important feature of this type of society is the autonomy of function of its structures. Probably this is what has served to allow Asian society to be defined as "feudal." Form prevailed over essence, over the forms of property as means of production and the social status of the primary producer.

Table 2 (on page 14) shows how these structures operated both before and after the revolution. But the many levels of Asian society, which are in many ways illusory, do not reflect this. The basis of Asian society is the community,[5] the foundation of which is the irrigation system (which in fact belongs to the government) and the private ownership of land by the *dekhan,* or peasant. Although land may be freely alienated from a particular owner (or user), it cannot be alienated from irrigation—that is, from the community as the collective user of the irrigation system.

In short, we have two levels of owners, the state and the community, and the boundaries between their domains are fairly arbitrary. In societies in which agriculture is based on artificial irrigation, the community is indifferent to the form of government and bureaucracy that creates the conditions for the functioning of the irrigation system. The main thing is the preservation of the internal structure of the community. The outer forms of such societies can vary,[6] but the essence remains identical. If the basis of the community remains *in essence* a combination of communal "ownership" (or use) of water and monopolistic private ownership by one family (large or small) of the irrigated land, then, notwithstanding any changes, the mahalla community will form and begin to function.

Traditionalism as a form of social and economic organization of society, juridical organization, and so forth, to a great degree corresponds to this means of production. This is true not just of the agricultural part of Central Asian society but of livestock breeders as well, independently of the manner in which livestock breeding is carried out. The only difference is that in place of irrigation there are communal grazing grounds, and instead of irrigated land, livestock.

Just before the Soviet period began in Central Asia, the socioeconomic structure of the region had two constituents. In the khanates of Khiva and Kokand and the emirate of Bukhara, the way of life was Islamic.[7] In the other part of Central Asia, which was under Russian control, the traditional governmental structure had been usurped by the Russian colonial administration, which concerned itself with questions of irrigation and regulation of pasture use. But colonial rule did not touch the essential aspects of social organization there, the traditional society. During the short period of its existence in Central Asia, capitalism was not

Table 2

Forms of Land Ownership and the Basic Structure of Power at the Mahalla Level of the Kishlak

Prerevolutionary Islamic state	Soviet state
Forms of land ownership and forms of taxes	
1. State land, or khan's land (nominally), in fact community land. Tax is part of harvest, or tax on production.	1. State land, on kolkhoz and sovkhoz (in fact). Fixed tax (in form of government economic plan).
2. Rented land (from the state or a private owner). Tax is part of harvest, or tax on production.	2. Rented land (from kolkhozes and sovkhozes). Tax is a fixed part of harvest.
3. Private land (*mullq*). Tax on production.	3. Personal land allotment (in fact, private). A fixed tax in cash for the land.
4. Pasture land, community held, untaxed. The shepherd is paid and there is a tax on the livestock.	4. Pasture land, community held, untaxed. The shepherd is paid, and there is a tax on livestock in the form of insurance.
5. *Waqf* land (belonging to religious bodies). Untaxed.	5. *Waqf* land (belonging to religious bodies). Untaxed
Organs of administration (on *mahalla* level)	
Rais: overseer of Islamic way of life, official state representative. Function is to ensure observance of *shari'a* and to collect taxes.	*Neighborhood committee:* official state representative. Official function is to organize internal life of neighborhood. Actual function is to administer the social and spiritual life of neighborhood: oversee observance of Islamic way of life, form public opinion. The function of the *rais* is performed by the president of the committee.
Mullah: state servant, the *imam* of mosque. Function is to administer ideological life, collect taxes, conduct religious rituals, teach in the *maktab,* administer *waqf* properties.	*Mullah:* neighborhood religious authority, the *imam* of the mosque. Function is to administer religious life of society, collect taxes, keep the parish purse, teach in the *maktab,* administer *waqf* property.

able to dismantle the social structure, as happened in British India.[8] The limited measures that the Russian colonial administration took to preserve the natural resources of Central Asia affected only certain aspects of the functioning of the community. In areas under Russian administration the basis for "state" Islam was destroyed, meaning the old governing structure that had organized communities in large territories into one entity. In the destruction of the canonical form of uniting communities, a nucleus was preserved that was capable of regenerating the entire organism in favorable circumstances. Traditionalism was preserved as the community's social structure at the level of daily life, incorporating the village and all its features.

Depending upon the size of the rural population, there will be one or more neighborhood mahallas, as justification for which there are created discrete irrigation systems, some of them quite small. Neighborhoods are joined together into avlods or similar social entities made up of related families. An *avlod* is a group of related families who trace their origins to one ancestor in the male line. As early as the nineteenth century there were avlods that formed social groups from one large family and practiced a unified economic pursuit under the direction of a senior male—a father or grandfather. In its turn, the family in Central Asia took and continues today to take various forms, from the simple small (or "nuclear") family to large familial communities of complex structure.

Historical sources depict state Islam in the prerevolutionary period as a society based on the dogmas of the Koran and on the *sunna* (customs) and *hadith* (sayings) of Muhammad. Scholars have created the impression that there was a distinct "Islamic law," "Islamic way of life," "Muslim forms of property," "Islamic ideology," later "Islamic banks," and so on.[9] The isolation of everything Islamic from the non-Islamic has been emphasized. Everything non-Islamic comes from the *kafirs*, unclean nonbelievers, and cannot be accepted by Muslims. This situation is the fundamental ideological basis for rejection of innovation of whatever sort.

At the same time, another characteristic of Islam that is little noted by scholars and politicians is the adaptability of Islam as a system. For every dogma, the Koran provides an alternative that directly contradicts the norms and rules that modern "everyday" theology has declared to be obligatory for the Muslim. For example, the Koran recognizes only one holy place, the Ka'aba (in the courtyard of the great Mosque of Mecca), the main locus of Allah. But pre-Islamic cults, which occupy a large place in the daily life of Muslims, are also well known, and believers revere thousands of holy places—graves, cemeteries, stones, springs, mountains, caves, trees, and so on. Many such sites have been canonized by the clergy and pilgrimage to them is considered an obligation for the Muslim. A simple list of such sites in Central Asia alone would fill dozens of pages. Every rural settlement has at least one holy place, while many have several. Another example is dietary injunctions. According to some of the clergy, when a Muslim travels he is exempt from these, and he may be considered to be traveling as soon as he leaves his village. If the Muslim does not find "clean" food on his way, then he can eat "unclean." The sin is small and may be expunged with an extra prayer. There are many such examples.

The establishment of Soviet rule in Central Asia completely destroyed the "state" part of Islam, which meant that the system of uniting communities changed. Nevertheless the *organizational structure* of Central Asian society remained *structurally* familiar for a Muslim. Soviet rule replaced that of the khans, taking over the large irrigation systems. The Soviet government became the owner of the water and regulated its supply to the fields. This is critical to an agricultural economy, since the harvest depends entirely upon the amount of water supplied to the fields. Fertilizer and technology have an important impact, but the deciding factor continues to be water. The state built new canals, drainage equipment, and bridges, and repaired the old ones. The lesser irrigation systems remained the concern of the villages and mahallas, or the communities.

The structure of these was not destroyed. There was an equalizing redistribution of land within the community, but the means of agriculture remained the same. Land collectivized into the *kolkhoz* (collective farm) was seen as governmental (it formerly had been the land of the khan), while the collective farm member's private plot was and is seen as *mullq,* or private property. At the village level the earlier forms of property essentially remained, with the sole difference that now this property was guaranteed by the government. Uniting the dekhans into brigades and teams did not destroy the old forms, since production subunits were formed along familial, neighborly, or tribal lines (meaning those of the mahalla).

This situation was precisely identified in the village of Avchi, in Ganchin Raion of Leninabad Oblast. Initially thirteen collective farms were established there, based on the number of avlods. Later these avlods were made into brigades and teams of one farm; moreover, in distributing personal-use plots to collective farm workers (meaning land that was irrigated before Soviet power), the boundaries of the old "tribal" and "avlod" holdings were strictly observed. "Alien" land could be occupied only after completing a buy-sell ritual, even if only formal and symbolic, or if it was bestowed as a gift. All of these acts of conveyance of "old" land were carried out (and still are) in the presence and with the participation of an unofficial mullah, following the norms of the *adat* (customary law) and *shari'a* (religious Islamic law). This situation is characteristic of urban as well as rural locales. Instances of the symbolic buying and selling of plots assigned by the city soviets for construction of individual houses were frequent, for example, in Leninabad in the 1950s. The "purchase" was abrogated only when a land owner had no "legal" heir. The urban mahalla strictly observed these norms. Such practices are preserved in rural locales even now.

Soviet scholars take little account of the specifics of Central Asia (the same is also true, incidentally, of the Caucasus). Traditionalism has once again begun to be manifested quite openly, as a petit bourgeois mode of production.[10] It is true, of course, that the forms of its manifestation are somewhat changed. The "secular" or "ritualistic" aspect has receded, and now the political aspect has come to the fore, in preservation of old "traditional" ways and practices. Opposition to the development of society has become the major concern of the "new" traditionalism.

This was first observed during the 1916 Uprising, which occurred during World War I.[11] In 1916 the Russian colonial government infringed on old practices when it tried to draft Muslims for work in labor brigades, provoking an uprising in the Central Asian territory under Russian control. Some historians' attempts to explain this movement as "antifeudal" will not withstand serious criticism. The uprising did not spread to the territory of the Islamic governments of Central Asia, to the emirate of Bukhara and the Khivan khanate, which those same historians characterize as "feudal and despotic." The anti-Russian and anticapitalist character of this movement is plain. In the majority of locales the rebels were led by clergy, and their main slogan was the rejection of everything progressive, of "kafir" or foreign innovation, both of which were identified with the Russians. There was action against the "feudal lords" only when these lords sided with the Russian administration.

This was the beginning of the Basmachi, or Freemen's, revolt, which abated somewhat after the overthrow of the tsar in February 1917 but flared up with new force after the October Revolution, when the Soviet government liquidated private property in the means of production and took the first steps to redistribute land and livestock.* The inspirers of this movement were always the Islamic clergy; the *kurbashi*, or leaders, simply carried out their will. An example of this is the cleric Karakum-ishan, who was the ideological inspiration for the bands of Jungid Khan, the great Turkmen kurbash. According to some accounts, Karakum-ishan was their actual leader. Only the extreme measures that

---

*There was resistance to Bolshevik rule throughout most of rural Turkestan from 1918 to 1920. (Turkestan was the prerevolutionary name for territory south of the Kazakh Steppe, including the Syr Daria and Semireche oblasts of today's Kazakhstan, and Kyrgyzstan, Uzbekistan, Tajikistan, and part of Turkmenistan.) After the unification of Turkestan with Russia, the resistance was gradually put down, although in places it remained a threat to Bolshevik rule until 1924. Most sources state that the resistance was completely defeated by 1936, but Poliakov's account puts it several years later.

Soviet authorities took in the 1930s liquidated the main forces of the Basmachi. Nevertheless, the Basmachi movement continued until the end of 1941. Participants of battles with the Basmachi saw vigorous Basmachi activity not just in remote regions of the Pamirs, but also, for example, in the Asht Raion of Leninabad Oblast in Tajikistan, where a band of Basmachi were partly routed, then dispersed, in October 1941.

The period of collectivization in the 1930s was also a stage in the struggle with tradition, but outwardly at least it proceeded more calmly. This was a time when traditionalism, defeated politically and militarily, became less active and began to adapt itself to new conditions.

The severe measures of the wartime period (1941–45) suppressed the old ways even more, so that even the most elementary rituals were not observed. In Turkmenistan, for example, *sunnat* (circumcision) was forbidden by law, and party members were punished for participating in funerals in which Islamic clerics took part. Furthermore, the rule that had been established during the civil war and the battle against the Basmachi was still closely observed: whoever was a defender of the old ways was an enemy of the people. Traditionalism and anti-Sovietism were synonymous.

The stronger Soviet power became, the more illusory was the idea of restoring Islamic statehood. Traditionalism survived at the level of the kishlak, and its renaissance came together with the resurrection of a folk economy. Traditionalism did not go beyond the bounds of the kishlak, and there was no information about it. Furthermore, for completely incomprehensible reasons the opinion formed—an opinion that unfortunately still is prevalent—that traditionalism does not exist even as an idea. In the USSR traditionalism is understood only as a religious ideology that finds expression in visits to "state" mosques by "people of the older generation" and "certain groups of the population." We have neglected traditionalism and let it develop to a dangerous level; it is important therefore to understand the basis on which it is built.

II

ECONOMIC BASES OF TRADITIONALISM

4

Traditionalism and the Economic Structure

Deal not unjustly, and ye shall not be dealt with unjustly.
The Koran, II, 279

Every phenomenon has a material—or, more precisely, an economic—basis. No social phenomenon exists outside of material production. As Karl Marx wrote, "The economic structure of society in any given epoch forms the real foundation which in the end explains the entire superstructure of legal and political institutions, just as it does the religious, philosophical, and other views of every historical period."[12] In this sense, for example, the thesis that there are no "roots" for religion in our society is unfounded. There have been no serious attempts to study the Central Asian way of life and explain not only the real reasons for its existence but also the mechanism of its transmission from one generation to another in the republics of Central Asia.

Analysis of the data reveals that at present the rural economy of Central Asia has two parts (see Figure 1). The first is the state sector, which has an industrial basis and is regulated by the state. Its lowest structural level is the collective farm (*kolkhoz*) or state farm (*sovkhoz*). The entire activity of the state sector is fixed in various documents and has been studied by numerous scholars. However, in light of the scandals of recent years,* it is now no

---

*Poliakov is referring to the cotton scandals in Uzbekistan. It has been revealed that in the late 1970s and early 1980s local party officials were involved in a multi-million-ruble scheme to falsify cotton production figures.

secret that even for this sector, previous official information about the economy of the Central Asian republics is quite far from representing reality. Nevertheless, by using the reports of regulatory bodies, mathematical methods, and other means, it is possible to obtain a more or less accurate picture of the state of the economy. Official information about automobile transport and the industrial cooperatives is less reliable, for there are many loopholes for private enterprise.

The second part of the rural economy is what is called the private economy of the collective and state farm members. The government does not regulate production on family plots, nor does it oversee it or study it. Because of the specifics of Central Asian conditions, this economy plays a very large role in the life of the population, as foreign scholars of Central Asia have noted. These conditions are defined primarily by geographic factors. The inequality, or, more precisely, unequal importance, of the two sectors that comprise the well-being of the rural family—the state sector being the job in a collective or state farm, and the private sector, work in a garden plot or on land rented from the government (the relationships depicted in Table 3)—is especially evident here, because the value of the second significantly exceeds the first.

The climatic conditions of the region permit the cultivation of agricultural products that do not grow in other parts of the country, and trade in them yields a very large profit (differential rent, type I); in this case the surplus value created in rural economies comes from the better and more easily accessible lands.

The great variety of natural climatic zones creates conditions for the cultivation in some parts of Central Asia of crops that are scarce in the region as a whole. This is especially true of potatoes, which in recent decades have become an important part of the food supply for the majority of the Central Asian population. At the same time, centralized distribution of this vegetable to the population is plainly inadequate, and the same is true for carrots. Nor are these the only examples, although unfortunately not all of the crops that are cultivated have food value. In recent years a

Table 3

Private Control of Land by Rural Residents

Personal land allotments	Rented land	Pasturage
Fully private property.	Temporary use by agreement.	Right (as a member of the community) to pasture privately owned livestock.
May be fully "alienated."	May not be "alienated" (but may be subleased).	
May be bequeathed.	May not be bequeathed.	May be bequeathed.
Has a fixed tax.	Fixed portion of harvest turned over.	Fixed per head fee to the shepherd.
Size limited by law.	Size not limited by law.	
May be enlarged by "reclamation" or "purchase."	Plot size may be increased through rental agreement.	
Minimum plot size: 0.15 hectare.*		
Maximum (fixed) plot size: 4 hectares.	Maximum (fixed) plot size: 5 hectares.	Maximum (fixed) herd size: 370 sheep.
Average plot size varies by region and crop.	Average plot size varies by region and crop.	Minimum herd size is the maximum possible for each region.

*A hectare equals 10,000 square meters, or a little less than 0.4 square mile.

large part of private-plot planting (and not only private-plot) has been devoted to plants that contain narcotic substances. The most important of these is a special sort of tobacco from which a narcotic called *nas-vai* is prepared (a tobacco that the "smoker" keeps under his tongue).

At present, the private agricultural economy of collective and state farm members tends to be commodity-based and, with some small exceptions, plays little part in providing the family with the types of produce they use. The economy is oriented primarily to the market. In mountainous and desert regions this economy is augmented or wholly replaced by commodity livestock breeding, primarily the raising of sheep for meat. In some regions the breeding of angora goats has become widespread in recent decades. This form of livestock breeding is wholly of a commodity type, and its products are not even partially used in the home. In addition to the herd's value as commodity, in mountainous, steppe, and desert regions the herd is also a form of accumulated wealth, meaning riches withdrawn from circulation.

As was noted, the government does not regulate private production, and the processes occurring in this sector of the rural economy of Central Asia are not studied or described (although Lenin saw enormous value in information about the peasant economy when seeking to understand both economic and political situations).[13] Ethnographers have a great unfulfilled responsibility to the government, although it is difficult to say how this situation came about. In private conversations scholars will justify the absence of studies about the real contemporary peasant economy by citing the complexity and delicacy of the topic, the lack of a developed working method, and so on, but in fact this is simply avoidance of one of the most pressing problems of our day, which no complexities or difficulties can justify.

Contemporary family production among the rural population of Central Asia, as has been pointed out, is primarily conducted on a relatively small plot of land worked without hired helpers; this is petty commodity, or petit bourgeois, production. Limitations on the dimensions of the land area make active use of technology unprofitable. As a rule, all work save plowing is done by hand. This creates the impression, especially among people unfamiliar with it, that this form of production, followed by sale of the product at the market and retention of the profit received, is an entirely familial business, with no relation to the state sector of the economy.

However, even the money received from marketing the product is not wholly consumed by the family; residents of the mahalla spend a significant portion of family income on various undertakings such as weddings and funeral feasts. For this reason, this form of production should not be called "individual." Its social dimension is evident, first of all, in conditions of artificially irrigated agriculture, which make individual family production impossible, unless of course the family is able to count upon scores of able-bodied men. The irrigation water for collective and state farm workers' private plots comes from equipment maintained (with some rare exceptions) by the government. The modern irrigation systems that deliver water to the field demand constant attention, and this is even more true of traditional systems. Both have to be kept clean of silt, and the devices that divert water from the streams into the irrigation ditches must be maintained and repaired. All this requires specialists of many types.

In the second place, working the land—plowing and harrowing—is done with state-owned farm machinery in return for a fee that is quite small (when compared with government expenditures). It should be noted that often even this small payment is not made when the machine operator is a family member. Only harvesting and processing of the harvest are done using the labor of family members alone, although even here we have found instances of the use of hired labor.

Sale of the product relies particularly heavily on the use of government property. Government transport is used, in all its forms and on favorable terms, as are the state's roads, which are of course free. Transportation of agricultural products is very simple; once loaded, the freight is guarded, for a symbolic payment, and places for trade are provided. The only individual element of this system is acquisition of the profit, as may be seen in Figure 1.

The state sector of the family economy is clear-cut. Pay is given in accordance with the amount and the quality of labor expended. The sum earned is subject to income tax and there are deductions for social-service funds, which in this case provide irrigation equipment, energy, roads, transport, and other government services supplied to rural inhabitants.

28 ECONOMIC BASES OF TRADITIONALISM

Figure 1. **Family Agricultural Economy**

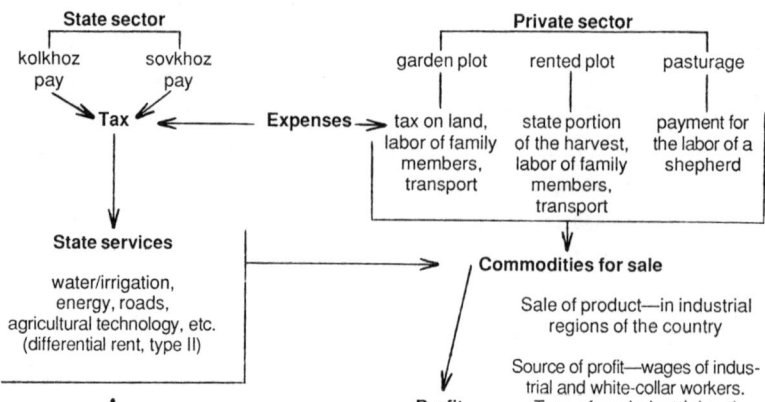

"Family" production is based on state-owned land that is allotted for private usage. There are three categories of such land: private plots (which are permanent), plots rented from the collective or state farm (temporary), and pastures. The legal status of these three types of land varies. Use of a private plot requires payment of a tax of one ruble per hundredth, which in Central Asia means fifteen rubles for 0.15 hectare. There is no additional payment for irrigation water for these plots. Payment to the state for rented land is in the form of a portion of the harvest grown on the land. Pasturage is free for the rural resident; he pays only for the labor of the herder. Expenses for the upkeep of private plots are insignificant in relation to the income that is obtained from them. In addition to the favorable circumstances provided by the government, incomes are further increased by frequent violations of the land regulations. In the mid-1980s, for example, in the kishlak of Pangaz in Asht Raion of Leninabad Oblast in

Tajikistan, one shepherd's private plot grew to four hectares. True, this is a unique instance, but plots of from a half to a full hectare are not rare even today.

The labor expended to get a unit of production and the market price of that unit are glaringly disproportionate. The price is always several times larger than the real labor expenditures. On the average in the regions studied by the expedition, in conditions of petit bourgeois production, the amount of yearly family income that was not subject to government tax was eight to ten thousand rubles. By itself the existence of so much money in large families might be welcomed, were it not for the methods by which it is acquired.

Growing any agricultural product, whether plant or animal, requires land. As has been noted, according to the rules set for Central Asia, the private plot of a rural inhabitant should not be larger than 0.15 hectare per family. In reality this rule is rarely observed, as there are several ways to increase a land allotment. The most common of these is early marriage. The married son's supposed separation from the family gives him the right to a land allotment. Another way is to buy land—or more exactly, to pay a bribe of the proper size to the person in charge of assigning land allotments. Some areas of Central Asia retain the right to "reclaimed" plots, to land that an individual has irrigated by his own efforts. It must also be remembered that from the moral viewpoint of society in the kishlak (or, among the Kirgiz and the Kazakhs, in the *aul*), all these methods are legal in that they are sanctioned by shari'a and adat law.

After the harvest is gathered, the product is processed and stored in a barn, and the time for sale of the goods is chosen. There is no need here for close examination of the details of this process, nor for analysis of all the factors that define it. It is worth noting, however, that this process illustrates well the fact that the entire economy is market-based, that labor is for the marketplace. The private plot is not a supplementary supplier of the family's requirements for agricultural products, as the government intended it should be when supplying the land allotments, but rather a source of income.

It is precisely this that motivates the collective or state farm member to enlarge his land allotments. It is also significant that this income is not subject to taxes but passes completely into the family budget. There is no sale of "surplus agricultural products" in the collective farm market here because in fact everything that is produced is "surplus." This is not a chance process; it is well established and cannot be called anything other than petit bourgeois, exhibiting all the sins of this means of production.

First among these sins is extremely irrational exploitation of the land. In petty commodity production there can be no discussion of preservation of the environment. Repeated planting of the same cultivars generally depletes the soil. Lack of plant rotation and the catastrophically ignorant use of artificial fertilizers leads to outright destruction of the soil. A vivid illustration of this are the settlements of Metk and Rosrovut, on the upper reaches of the Aksu River (Ganchin Raion in Tajikistan). For decades the potato was the main crop here, planted on at least 80 percent of the cultivated land, including all irrigated private plots. The rest of the irrigated land was planted with carrots. Ten or fifteen years ago the potato harvest was 60 tons per hectare; now the harvest has fallen to 15–20 tons.

A similar situation obtains with apricot orchards. Old trees do not give big crops, but replacing them with young trees is undesirable in the private-plot economy, because income will fall significantly or ceases entirely until the new trees reach fruit-bearing age. There are no plots available on which a scientifically based orchard economy might be introduced. At the same time, the prosperity of a very large number of rural families depends *entirely* on precisely this sort of "private-plot" economy.

Unfortunately, the executive organs of the local governments do not always make correct decisions appropriate for local conditions. Land allotments above regulation size are supposed to be removed from private usage, which creates an extremely tense situation. Solving all these problems involves many difficulties.

The tensions are not identical everywhere, since the same causes have different effects in every kishlak. This is not a phenomenon simply of the present. The peculiarities of economic activity in each region (which sometimes consist of several kishlaks) were established rather long ago, and drastic changes in the economic situation cannot be made painlessly. In the context of today it is not the economic aspect of this tension that comes to the fore, but the political aspect, which needs to be examined.

5

Commercial Operations

> *Many of them dost thou see, racing each other in sin and rancour, and their eating of things forbidden.*   The Koran, V, 65

The first political aspect of the petty commodity economy might conditionally be called "external." The trader—a role that might be played by virtually any adult male—is very often not the person who has produced his goods. He seeks his pickings not among his own rural ("Islamic") society, where he lives and where the process of production occurs, but among the population of the industrial regions. Products are sold many hundreds or thousands of kilometers from the place of production. Nor does he scruple to stay outside of the "Muslim world." The nationality, religion, or social class of the buyer is not important—only income is. When dealing in scarce goods, the seller determines the price. This conflict-rich situation of buying and selling occurs not in the environment where the trader lives and works, but outside of it. At home the seller is a dekhan, a worker, regardless of the nature and conditions of labor and of production as a whole.

In that part of modern Central Asian society which pursues petty commodity production, income produced by any means is respected as beneficent and is approved by public opinion. It should be noted here that we have paid and still pay too little attention to this contact between the opposing sides, the "rural seller" and the "industrial buyer," or the exploiter and the exploited. This contact—the act of buying and selling—is of short duration, and in practice is *always* to the advantage of the seller.

Ethnic or national questions are another aspect of the problem. Data from the expedition and my own observations at various markets in Central Asia, the Russian Federation, and the Baltic republics, as well as conversations on the subject with a very wide circle of people, suggest that for the majority of customers a Central Asian and a speculating profiteer are synonymous. This is particularly dangerous on the everyday level. "Everybody in Central Asia is rich," "They've all got bags of money," and other such clichés do nothing to improve interethnic relations and make it difficult to explain to people that it is wrong to confuse the profiteer with the collective farm member who is selling his own goods. Since the price each of them charges for dried apricots is identically high, how is this problem to be solved?

According to our informants, in the late 1980s it became much more difficult for Central Asians to sell goods outside of their republics. Cases of sellers being robbed have become more common. How widespread this phenomenon may be is difficult to judge, but many commodity producers who used to market their goods themselves have begun to turn more often to the services of buyers in the villages and middlemen in the markets. Here is where the second actor in the petty commodity economy, the middleman who accumulates the product, assumes real importance. The middleman is the main competition for the state cooperatives, which are government organizations. The middleman pays more for a kilogram of dried apricots than the state cooperative does. With the significant volume of goods to be purchased—each household has no fewer than 400–500 kilograms of produce—the difference in price is noticeable, more than 1,000 rubles. The state loses in this competition, and the middleman flourishes, buying goods from the primary rural producer at the site of production (in the kishlak) or at the bazaar. The price that the middleman pays for a commodity, such as apples, when he buys them from the peasant or dekhan, is significantly lower than the price for which he sells them at the bazaar.

Middlemen, joined together into a sort of society, monopolize the trade in certain goods. This leads to the prices for the goods that they sell being set solely for the benefit of their society. The nature of the middleman in the peasant economy was fully exposed by Lenin.[14] It needs only to be noted here that a middleman is to be found in practically every settlement, although it is not essential that the middleman be a resident of the place where he is buying. For example, the residents of Chorku kishlak (in Leninabad Oblast, Tajikistan) "service" the neighboring Kirgiz villages.

In September 1986, in an effort to regulate illegal trade, a number of places forbade the "independent" export of agricultural products; in response to this, all trading arrangements were halted, as a political gesture. For example, no dried apricots of any sort (neither *uriuk*, which are dried with the pits still in them, nor *koriaga*, which are pitted) were taken to the markets of Leninabad from the raions of Asht or Isfara. Undoubtedly this situation upset city-dwellers, making them unhappy with the new state of the peasant market.

In 1985 the price of a ton of dried apricots in the markets of Moscow and Moscow Oblast averaged around 8,000 rubles. In 1988 the price rose to 12,000 rubles a ton. It might seem that the original producer of the goods makes the greatest profit from the price rise. By using a middleman, he has no risk of a loss at the market, and thus can raise the initial price. However, the real price at the market is set by the middlemen, who are organized into a corporation, which makes them in essence monopolists in the sale at the bazaar of goods produced by the dekhan or private farmer. As a rule, the middleman sets the prices not only for the goods he buys from the dekhan but also for those that he sells to him. Manufactured goods that the dekhan needs for national rituals have also risen in price at the fairs. Demand is greatest for certain fabrics used for making dresses, "national" scarves of Japanese manufacture, and so on. Speculators create artificial shortages of these goods, so that the prices for them are two to three times higher than the state price. Instead of a twofold increase, the dekhan now pays threefold. In practice, the producer is left with the same sum as in the past, and the benefit goes to other actors.

In its entirety, the process of distribution of income received in the private economy in the mid- and late–1980s had several variants (Table 4). The first is that the producer himself sells what he produces. A second is that a middleman and seller intervene between producer and customer. A third is that in the process of marketing, the cooperatives will come into play. In addition, the products gotten from the various types of land—the private plot, rented land, and pasturage—will have peculiar characteristics.

In practice, the second variant was predominant. The first occurred rather rarely (for large consignments of goods), and the third, with the participation of the cooperatives, almost never. As for the livestock trade, the owner of the livestock almost always sold his animals as live weight and split the income with the meat middleman from the bazaar. In reality the producer in the existing system received less than 40 percent of the market price of the goods. The remainder was left to the middleman, the salesman, and the bazaar. Totaling all forms of goods (fruits, vegetables, and livestock), the bazaar got about 30 percent of the market price. (See Table 5.)

If cooperatives were to replace the middlemen, even if prices were to remain as high as those presently set by the private middlemen, the profit for the government, and thus for the population, would be enormous. Speculators would lose their initial capital. It would be worth discussing the possible consequences of such an action separately, but in any event it is plain that the system that existed through the late 1980s for dividing the profit received from the economy of the dekhans had nothing whatever to do with socialism.

In addition to the grower-seller, the middleman, and a whole range of secondary people (the racketeers), the transporter has a large role in the process under discussion. No matter how optimistic reports may be that transport of freight is being controlled, some loophole for the enrichment of individual drivers always remains. Of course, some of the measures taken in the last few years have complicated the unsupervised use of state freight trucks (although not of other vehicles) in the petty commodity

Table 4

Distribution of Income and Expenditures of the Private Economy

Land	Means of sale of production	Distribution of expenditures					Distribution of income					Frequency of expenditures			Frequency of income					
		Cost of production		Taxes															
		Transport	Storage	Monetary	Part of harvest	Payment for pasturage	P	M	S	B	C	P	M	C	P	M	S	B	C	
Private	P	P	P	P			+	−	−	+	−	15	4	5	9	3	6	6	3	With participation of the cooperative in the sale of production
	M	M	M	P			+	+	+	+	−									
	B	C	C	P			+	−	+	−	+									
Rented	P	P	P		P		+	−	−	+	−	12	4	−	−	6	3	3	6	Without participation of the cooperative in the sale of production
	M	M	M		P		+	+	+	+	−									
	B	C	C		P		+	−	+	−	+									
Pasturage	P	P				P	+	−	−	+	−									
	M	P				P	+	+	+	+	−									
	B	C				P	+	−	+	−	+									

Key: P producer; M middleman; C cooperatives; S seller; B bazaar; + receives income; − does not receive income.

Table 5

Division of Income from Sale of Commodities at the Peasant Market
(direct vs. secondary participants)

	1985		1988	
	in %	in rubles	in %	in rubles
Producer (dekhan)	36.5	2,920	50.0	6,000
Middleman	36.5	2,920	29.0	3,500
Seller	9.0	720	9.0	850
"Bazaar"	18.0	1,440	12.0	1,650
of which:				
overhead	12.5	1,000	8.0	1,115
"insurance"	5.5	440	4.0	535

economy, but these measures are plainly insufficient. As long as there is uncontrolled transportation "on the side," there is also the possibility of uncontrolled income. The cost of transport has risen because the risk has risen; as we know, everything must be paid for.

In recent years the participation of secondary people has become much more noticeable. Rackets have not become as obvious a phenomenon as they have among the cooperatives, but they still sometimes show their claws, at least where Central Asian goods are concerned. The field data show, however, that the rackets are wholly subordinate to the corporations of middlemen; rackets are their weapon against people trying to go it alone, without them. It should be stressed again that public opinion in the kishlak and aul approves, or at least does not condemn, all commercial activities, no matter what their relationship to socialist legal norms; public opinion accepts them unconditionally as "Muslim." Lenin himself wrote of the "ruble-determined" morality of petty commodity production.[15]

The second political aspect of the petty commodity economy could be called "internal." Like the first part, it has several facets. Deregulation or "destatization" in the economic sphere has an impact on an entire way of life that, as has been mentioned, even today is wholly defined by shari'a, disguised as "national traditions" at the family, neighborhood, and village level. The timid experiments made in some places to change the way of life have so far not affected the economy. Only the form has changed, while the essence of the phenomenon has remained the same.

The most vivid expression of the "internal" part of the political aspect is found in the true demographic situation in Central Asia, where very large families are a source of tension. While I do not wish to generalize or make sweeping criticisms of how the fight against illegal income is being conducted locally, it does seem that those responsible fail to appreciate the full complexity of the situation. Our salaries in the state sector are not set in a way that permits a working father to feed (or keep) seven or eight dependents on what he is paid. If a family is denied a supplemental source of material prosperity, which in this case is really its primary source, the question of how people are to go on living will become uppermost. The traditional way of life—or, more precisely, the way of life sanctioned by Islam—demands large expenditures, which from our point of view are irrational, on traditional rituals (not to be confused with religious ones). The social and political consequences of cutting off this unearned income might not appear in full force in the first year, and would probably take a certain period of time, but we must be aware that there would be an immediate social reaction to such changes. In any case, hostility toward the policies of the Soviet authorities are exacerbated by such traditionalist statements as "The authorities don't let us live in our own way, in the Muslim way," which our materials indicate come from the "unofficial" clergy.

6

Demographics and Employment

*All that hath been promised unto you will come to pass:
Nor can ye frustrate it.*   The Koran, VI, 134

The demographic factor is primary for the family economy and for the entire rural economy. In Central Asia manual labor is the main form of work in family production and in public production of the great majority of agricultural crops, with the exception of grains and hay. This is particularly evident in the final stage of the agricultural cycle, the gathering of the harvest. The principal crop of Central Asia—cotton—demands a large amount of manual labor in the harvesting; fruits, grapes, and vegetables are cultivated almost entirely by hand. The number of machines used in harvesting them is insignificant. Be that as it may, it is impossible to guarantee even a minimally satisfactory employment rate among the population in public production in the state economy. The demographic situation in Central Asia thus aggravates the political elements of economic activity in the village. It should be noted that the least labor in family production falls to the head of the family; as a rule, men are occupied in trade and procurement of scarce goods.

A few years ago, in the late 1970s, both scholarly literature and the general press vigorously condemned a "demographic explosion" that was supposed to be occurring in Central Asia. However, materials gathered from archives, in the field, and drawn from other works convincingly suggest that no such explosion has occurred. In reality what has occurred is one of the natural consequences of development in Asian society and of the materialist dialectic: quantitative changes have produced a qualitatively new condition for society. More specifically, it may be said with complete confidence that it was appending the region to Russia that created conditions for an increase in the population. We have studied this question in particular detail in the area that today is Leninabad Oblast in Tajikistan. From 1870 to 1931 the population increased 3.5 times,[16] while by 1980 it had increased 10.5 times. To anticipate a bit, such figures should demonstrate the scholarly dubiousness and political fallaciousness of the argument that the people of Central Asia, being "peripheral," "died out" after the region was joined to Russia.

In the 1940s, and especially in the 1950s, textbooks and popular literature spoke insistently of the responsibility borne by the Russian people for the exploitation of the Central Asian peoples by the Russian colonial regime. The Russian people were thus accused of acting in concert with tsarism. By itself this idea is not only absurd, but also dangerous, in that everything that is socially, politically, economically, or culturally negative in the Central Asian region is attributed to "the arrival of the Russians."

This population growth is not a "demographic explosion;" What happened is that in the first stage, 1870–1931, the major cause of population growth in the region was political stability and the end of internecine war. Stability immediately affected life expectancy, increasing it, which in turn brought a growth in the number of married couples, which is partially reflected in the growth in the number of households. As far as it is possible to judge from the results of studies of excavated graves, there was no noticeable lowering of infant mortality, as compared to the period before absorption by Russia. As a rule, for each adult grave there were four to seven children's graves.

The second stage, from 1931 to the present, is characterized by greater significance of social and political factors. Infant mortality has dropped sharply because of a rise in the standard of living, free medical care, and a whole range of other conditions. In surveying the causes of population growth, it is also necessary to recall a specifically Central Asian factor: marriage is obligatory for people of both sexes who have reached actual (physiological) marriageable age. Now the proper form of state registration of marriages exists in rural areas just as it does in cities (even if it is still far from what it should be), but fifteen or twenty years ago actual marriage, performed according to shari'a law, took place well before young people achieved eighteen years of age. The social morality that says that the more children one has, the better, must also be remembered. Artificial termination of pregnancy is forbidden by shari'a law. The reason given for why a large number of children is desirable is always the same: the economic benefit of a large number of working hands in family agriculture. This brings up one of the most important problems of modern Central Asian society—child labor, which will be discussed below.

All of these conditions have created an extraordinarily complex demographic situation of absolute and relative overpopulation. The complexity is worsened by the very small, even insignificant flow of rural population to the cities. The cause of this phenomenon will also be investigated below.

An enormous number of the rural population (which is the great majority of the total population of the Central Asian republics and largely indigenous to the region) take no part in public production. In some regions the proportion of the population not employed in the state sector approaches eighty percent.

This situation has arisen, first and foremost, because the sharp rise in population has been accompanied by greatly inadequate growth of both the rural and the urban economies. While the population of Leninabad Oblast has increased 10.5 times, the amount of land under cultivation has increased only 2.5 times. The situation in Leninabad Oblast is all the more alarming, since in comparison with most other regions of Central Asia, the geographic and economic situation here is quite favorable. Located in the western part of the Fergana valley, the oblast contains the most important industrial region of Tajikistan. The region is well supplied with water (in comparison to other regions), the communications network is well developed, there is a great deal of pasturage and arable land, and there are useful mineral deposits. Nevertheless, the employment figures for the population leave a great deal to be desired.

The native population, both Uzbeks and Tajiks, is enormously difficult to resettle in the cities. Furthermore, the growth cited above is only for the flat areas of the oblast; in the mountainous and foothill areas the amount of irrigated land has significantly decreased, primarily due to disruptions in the water cycle that are the result of man's activity. In the mountains, where there is an extraordinarily great shortage of arable land, fields that have been irrigated since time immemorial are now planted in dryland conditions (because of a lack of water). This greatly reduces their yield. However, it is not just the settled peoples that have increased the population density; the settlement of nomadic livestock-breeding peoples in the oases, a process that continued until the 1930s, removed large areas of pasture lands from economic use, which in essence intensified the land shortage.

The complexity of the situation may be seen in the case of Karl Marx State Farm in Ganchin Raion of Leninabad Oblast. On the territory of the farm there are 20,000 people, with a working-age population of 9,000, and 650 jobs (the figures are for 1984). A certain portion of the male population is employed in the nonproductive sphere, in schools, communications, state trade, and so on, but these are no more than 500–600 people. The remainder, just under 8,000 people, work in the private economy.

Women are almost entirely excluded from public production, in the first place because of their many children, in the second because of the lack of jobs, and in the third because of tradition, or more precisely, shari'a. Islamic law does not approve of men and women working together in the same building, or of girls leaving home to get advanced education or training. Traditional law (a synthesis of shari'a and common law) does not sanction disruption of the family foundations; children (especially girls) must be either with their parents or in their own families.

Thus, if women are taken into account, more than 85 percent of the adult population is forced to work in private petty commodity production. Nevertheless, all of the adult married males, whether or not they are working in the state sector, are considered to be state farm workers and are given private plots, which they have acquired in one of the ways outlined above. The attempts of some of our critics to explain this situation as the result of the farm's concentration on livestock breeding, which traditionally does not require large numbers of hands, does not hold up.

Here I should explain in a little more detail about the investigation of the combined Central Asian expedition and the place of field materials in the general system of proof. As soon as we discovered the situation described above, a program was immediately elaborated to study it. This became the subject of a doctoral dissertation by one of the members of the expedition. Much archival material was also used, and the ethnographic team studied this problem over a period of three years. With the assistance of the statistical methods worked out on the expedition, this region (the northern slopes of the central part of the Turkestan chain) was studied in detail, and economic and cultural zoning was done.

These expedition studies have shown that in this region farming traditionally played and continues to play the same role as livestock breeding, indeed perhaps a greater one. However, in modern conditions farming cannot absorb the entire working-age population. A special study of this was conducted at a stock-breeding sovkhoz in Osh Oblast of Kirgizia, where the population had gone over to farming. The picture there was as follows. Although there was a general labor surplus, there was at the same time a shortage of workers in the vineyards. The infrastructure of the economy is such that it is unprofitable to work continuously in the state sector.

Minimum participation in field work on the state farm is undertaken solely to obtain a plot of private land. Contracts for tobacco crops are not even taken by Kirgiz, but by "immigrant" Tajiks. People only enter the public sector (as contract laborers) when they have to earn money to pay for a ritual of some sort, or to buy some large item. Specific situations, although they have a similar character, take on a number of particularities. Materials gathered in the regions of the Fergana valley, where agriculture has traditionally taken a leading role, show a similar situation. The surplus of workers there is as great as elsewhere.

The example of Karl Marx State Farm is not unique. The villages Pangaz and Varukh are in analogous natural conditions. In the first of these, which is situated in the Asht Raion of Leninabad Oblast, the population has increased more than eleven times in the space of a hundred years, so that 12,000 people now live in the village. Of this number, fewer than a 1,000 men and about 300 women work in the state sector. The women work making flat-weave rugs in a special workshop and at home. Most men work in the state farm only a month or two a year, often less. Nevertheless the official statistics include all of these under the rubric "state farm workers," creating the impression of full employment. The identical picture is to be found in the other village mentioned, Varukh, in Isfara Raion, as well as in the villages that we studied in Andijan Oblast, Uzbekistan.

The situation in cotton-growing regions is no less complex. The majority of the population in fact works in public production only part of the year, when cotton is picked. Mechanization of the majority of operations involved in cultivating this major Central Asian crop has freed a large number of hands. Here we once again witness the paradoxical situation of a surplus of local labor, while the farms must demand that additional labor resources be brought in from the city and from non-cotton regions (most often these are students).[17] At the same time a large part of the adult rural population is busy in private production.

Quite often this private production is disguised behind a family contract with the farm. A good undertaking frequently becomes the source of income and wealth. The harvest on rented land plots is two to three times greater than on collective or state farm lands. But it is the productivity of the farms that is used to measure units of production, on the basis of which the renter's payment to the state is calculated. Even now, very little attention is paid to the condition of land plots after renters have used them. No attention is paid to blatant exploitation and destruction of land, despite the fact that even without such waste the severe hunger for land grows worse.

In the period under study family size has changed sharply. In some regions family size reaches ten people for every one working in public production. Here is where the problem of providing for all those family members not working in the state sector is particularly acute. It is impossible to do so on the salary of the family head alone; it requires the labor of all members of the family. The more workers there are, the greater the land's yield, though this, too, is true only up to a certain point. However, the quantity of food that is sufficient to feed the family members is insufficient to assure the family's social life at the level of the mahalla and the kishlak. Government measures to limit non-labor income, for all their half-heartedness, create a complicated situation. Elimination of livestock in excess of legal norms and the removal of "excess" land plots from the family economy force the choice between two types of expenditures—those for the family, meaning children fed and clothed, and social expenditures, meaning those to satisfy the mahalla. The latter means satisfaction of traditionalism. In everyday life the family constantly scrimps in order to satisfy the various "social enterprises" of the mahalla, as a result of which the everyday needs of the family are always kept to a minimum. As a rule, this leads to social tension, since there are sharp inequalities of property among families and enormous difficulties for poorer families in undertaking the activities that bestow prestige.

7

Private Enterprise and Livestock

> *And do not eat up your property among yourselves for vanities, nor use it as bait for the judges.*   The Koran, II, 188
>
> *Do no mischief on the earth, after it hath been set in order.*
>   The Koran, VII, 56

Petty commodity production in Central Asia has to a large degree become private enterprise, leaving the boundaries of the village and penetrating the state sector of the economy and even the activities of the state organs. There is a continual disorganization of the economy, primarily of trade within the Soviet Union. The many middlemen (most of them strong young men) remove the best and scarcest goods from the state stores to offer them at the "peasant" market at profiteering prices. Shortages of goods are artificially created, the deficit to be satisfied by the black market. Traditional goods, which are essential components of the so-called national customs, are the first items to be affected by these organized deficits. Besides disrupting the economy, this drawing off of goods makes the workers lose faith in Soviet authority. Although income in this case is derived without the intervention of an exploiter in production, the exploitation of both the worker and the government, as a social organism, is obvious.

Bribes are widely used to guarantee the functioning of this system. The bribe is part and parcel of this way of life, and always has been. The concept of bribery as such does not exist in

Islam. Both the shari'a and public opinion regard bribes as payment for services rendered, that is, for the "work" that someone does to benefit the person requesting the service. The bribe is sanctified by tradition, and today, public opinion in the mahalla does not condemn bribery. It even makes no difference that a person in a responsible post gets a state salary for his work. For example, it is common practice that the president of the neighborhood committee (the mahalla) takes a fee when he signs and seals any document.

Unearned income is also defined by bribes, which are of enormous size, given the local standard of living. Bribes are no longer a one-time occurrence, but have become a steady means of support for people in authority. The dimensions of the financial operations of private entrepreneurs are very large. In many situations the sums involved are so great that the notes are not even counted; they are weighed on scales, or doled out in packets of large-denomination bills.* A bribe of 60,000 rubles is not considered extraordinary. Bribery is now the norm in all dealings, regardless of the position of the person in authority. It has become the practice to convey a bribe through an intermediary, sometimes a government figure. This creates the appearance of propriety for the bureaucrat taking the bribe.

Private enterprise cannot make open use of all its income, even more so cannot deposit it in a savings bank.† Instead, income is removed from circulation (and the economy), which freezes a large quantity of paper money.

Income from private enterprise is often converted to livestock. Our materials show that traditionalism in the livestock-breeding regions is constantly growing stronger. This process is accompanied by growth in the size of herds under private control. The size of private herds is such that at times these animals outnumber the state-owned herds. For example, in 1987 at the Frunze State Farm of Osh Oblast, in Kirgizia, there were 4,500 sheep in the state flock, but at least 20,000 head of sheep and goats in

---

*Fifty- and hundred-ruble notes were withdrawn from circulation in January 1991, in part to curb such practices nationwide.
†Soviet citizens had to demonstrate the source of bank deposits.

private flocks. The situation with cattle is analogous; the residents' herd is much larger than the state farm's. The income this livestock produces comes from state-owned irrigated pasture and the labor of herders. For example, in Ganchin Raion in Tajikistan, in some families the number of privately held livestock reaches 300 head or more. Also, in 1984 in the aforementioned Karl Marx State Farm, there were 50,000 sheep, but fodder was being stored for 52,500. Pasturage was also calculated for that same number of animals. To whom did the other 2,500 sheep belong?

In addition to having negative social consequences, the uncontrolled number of livestock and overgrazing do colossal damage to the environment. This has led to a deterioration of pasture conditions throughout Central Asia. In turn, destruction of the ground cover in mountainous regions (where pasturing livestock in the forests affects the ecological situation particularly adversely) has led to the creation of gullies of mud and rock, which form in mountain streams after rains or during rapid snow melt. Such gullies are enormously destructive. The most striking result of use of mountain pastures is in Leninabad Oblast of Tajikistan, where in 1987, for example, one-seventh of all settlements suffered from wash-outs from the mountains. These cause a great deal of economic damage to the population of the mountains, the foothills, and the plains. Overgrazing of the mountain forests has an extremely adverse effect on the hydrography of the region, which has already had a serious negative impact on various areas of the economy of Central Asia.

Unable to maintain the sort of varied herd that would cause less damage to pasturage than does a uniform herd, the private farm primarily keeps small animals—sheep and, in some regions, angora goats. Dairy cattle are secondary in number and significance. The market demand for this type of herd is clear. In today's conditions, herds in excess of the norm are viewed as necessary to the family economy, guaranteeing the family supply of meat. This is a very bad mistake. Accumulation of animals continues, even if to a somewhat lesser degree than before the new government measures to limit it. For example, herds belonging to people from Kyrgyzstan are pastured on the territory of Tajikistan, while Tajik sheep are pastured in Kyrgyzstan, and no record of these herds or their pasture is kept. This allows the private herder to keep a personal flock of more than 300 sheep, although the average household has thirty to fifty sheep. Nevertheless, despite the growth of herd sizes, the price of meat at the bazaars remains high, and the meat shortage grows worse, as a peculiar sort of monopoly of private meat production has evolved.

The trade in land plots is a direct threat to our society, because the only people who can become large land owners are those who have achieved their wealth by dishonest means. In today's conditions, honest workers cannot compete with swindlers. In regions where conditions are favorable for growing scarce crops (such as potatoes), land is transferred for bribes ("sold," in shari'a terms), a plot of 0.15 hectares going for 30,000 rubles (in 1983, in Ganchin Raion).

In another example of private enterprise from the same region, a certain Jumbai had on his payroll seven truck drivers, who are registered as government employees. He is one of the largest traders in livestock and potatoes in this region.

Private enterprise actively interferes in personnel policy, primarily in the police and the courts. Private entrepreneurs purchase their right to engage in illegal activities. Nor is the more usual sort of bribes overlooked. A one-time "contribution" can cover up crimes that should be punished by law. Thus, for example, in 1983 in Leninabad, a child was run over and killed by a drunk driver. The investigation proceeded in a very strange manner, and then, after the trial, at which the accused was sentenced to eight years in prison, the criminal did not serve a single day. Even the intercession of Moscow did not change the situation; and this criminal was just a simple meat-pie seller, from the city park. Traditionalism plays a leading role in situations of this sort; public opinion is shaped through the mahalla, which condones any actions by its adepts as long as they do not violate traditional norms. The discredit done to the Soviet government in such cases is obvious, as there is an antigovernment quality to this bribery.

III

TRADITIONALISM AND THE FAMILY

8

Central Asian Family Structure

> *Then strive together as in a race towards all that is good,*
> *wheresoever ye are.*   The Koran, II, 148

Petty commodity production also affects the organization of the family, which in Central Asian society depends entirely on the will of the parents. Young people make independent decisions about marriage only in extraordinary and very rare circumstances. The formation of a new family is always a planned event. The marriage couple is chosen extremely carefully, on both sides.

The initiative always comes from the family of the young man. The active search for a bride is undertaken by the mother, or, if she is not alive, by one of the closest female relatives, who must be elderly. Information about the proposed bride is gathered from the girl's neighbors and acquaintances. Very often (in certain places this is the rule) the bride-to-be is chosen from among the female relatives on the mother's side, or from a neighboring house. In this latter case too, especially in rural areas, there is generally some kind of blood connection; cross-cousin marriages are considered the most desirable. A "close" bride and her family are familiar to the groom's family, and hence significantly better.

The mother or the female relative who chooses the bride is in no way influenced by the tastes and desires of the young man, on the principle that "your elders know best what has to be done." The great majority of future husbands regard this manner of choosing a bride with equanimity, justifying it by saying that the bride will have to be in constant contact with her future mother-in-law. If the two women like one another, then the home will be peaceful. The bride of the youngest son is chosen with particular care, since he does not have even the formal right to leave his parents. He must live in his father's house, which he will inherit with all its property. Most often, however, all of the brides stay under one roof with the mother-in-law. Houses or rooms for the married sons are built alongside the father's house in the great majority of cases. The formal division of married sons into individual families is only done to get additional private garden plots.

Young people entering into marriage often do not see one another prior to registration in the marriage registry office. Before that, there is a form of introduction in which the girl is shown her "betrothed" when he is standing or strolling with his friends, on the other side of the street. The young man is "introduced" in the same way. In the Andijan Oblast of Uzbekistan we recorded instances of affianced pairs having been introduced through photographs.

There are cases of a girl having been shown the photograph of one man, whom she agrees to marry, and then a completely different person comes to the marriage registry office, often one with physical defects. As a rule, in such instances the girl marries anyway, since refusal to marry is forbidden by public opinion.

It is one of the most fearsome tragedies of Central Asia that the sole form of protest possible in these circumstances is self-immolation by the bride. This topic has already been discussed at some length in the popular press. I would only add that in addition to the 270 such self-immolations of which we know,* there are uncounted victims who have been swallowed up by, for example, the silent waves of the Zeravshan River. Also silent are official statistics on the number of women who have poisoned themselves with vinegar essence.

In the part of Central Asia we studied, the *kalym* (the bride-price paid by the groom) is widely observed; more precisely, this

---

*The figure of 270 self-immolations of young women in Uzbekistan in 1987 was reported in the Soviet press.

is the sale of young women. The genesis of this phenomenon, which is essentially the same as slave trafficking, is fantastically confused. Without going into an analysis of the scholarly discussions of the kalym,[18] I would point out that none of them explain why this ugly phenomenon continues.

It is incorrect to define the kalym as "a holdover of earlier social relations," as many Soviet sources do. The kalym is evolving and its dimensions are growing. Nor should the kalym be regarded as a "dangerous national tradition," for it has no national boundaries. Essentially this is a social phenomenon.

For example, over the past ten years the average amount of the kalym in Dushanbe (Tajikistan) has grown from 3,000–4,000 rubles to 10,000–12,000, or at least threefold. It must also be noted that the kalym occurs among workers as well, not just among peasants. One of the female workers of the Dushanbe satin factory sold her daughter in September 1984 for 12,000 rubles. The other women workers confirmed that the kalym is a common occurrence in their milieu.

The kalym is widespread in Turkmenistan and in southern Tajikistan; this is confirmed not only by materials from the expedition but also by accounts in the popular press. The kalym has grown particularly briskly in Turkmenistan, where it can reach 40,000 rubles. These problems in the republic were well illustrated in a *Pravda* article (29 March 1986) that examined the question of bride abduction. In addition to the juridical question of the violence being done to persons, this article also touched on the distress of the brides' parents, who, when their daughters are "stolen" with the girls' own consent, have been deprived of their kalym. Even party workers were among those who mourned their lost kalyms.

Like other such "holdovers," the kalym is made sacrosanct by tradition. The press, and the very small number of scholarly and popular works that have in one form or another mentioned the persistence of the kalym (and none of them have subjected the practice to serious criticism), all fail to pose the main question, which has to do with economic rationale. In the best of circumstances there is a kind of pointless fuming about how hard it is for the groom's family to accumulate the kalym; not only does this not touch on the essential problem, it obscures it further. The kalym, coming as it does at the very beginning of a new family's existence, already preordains a whole range of extremely negative phenomena and serves not only to stabilize traditionalism but even to strengthen it. The kalym degrades society as a whole.

After the birth of a boy, which in the condition of the hypertrophic fertility of Central Asian families cannot be called a rare event, money begins to be saved for the *sunnat-toi,* the celebration of his circumcision. Practice indicates that if circumcision is forbidden, as it was in Turkmenistan until 1989, then there is a sharp rise in the size of kalyms, so that the family's total expenditures remain high.

It should be remembered that the young rural family increases in number every one-and-a-half to two years. Living expenses rise, and the size of kalyms or the expenses of circumcision in the best of circumstances remain the same, or else grow larger. Saving the necessary sums is achieved primarily at the expense of grocery money. The appearance of a male child in the family thus exacerbates health problems for adults and children alike. A mother who has not received the necessary nourishment can neither give birth to nor feed a wholly viable infant.

The situation is made even worse by the fact that birthrates are not dropping but rising. For example, 25 percent of the women in the Andijan Oblast of Uzbekistan give birth twice in a single year, at the beginning and at the end. This significantly increases expenditures on rituals. There is a natural selection active in human society. For example, infant mortality in the Isfara Raion of Leninabad Oblast in 1983–84 was 52 per thousand; now this has dropped somewhat, to 48–50 per 1,000. In Asht Raion of the same oblast, where traditionalism is significantly weaker, mortality was 38 per 1,000. According to the statistics of the World Health Organization, infant mortality is considered critical when it reaches 40 deaths per 1,000. However, despite extremely high infant mortality, there is also significant population growth in

Central Asia. Some of the consequences of this growth have already been discussed.

The kalym is not the only expenditure in starting a new family. It is necessary to save large sums for conducting the wedding itself, with a feast, gifts for the relatives, and the bride's trousseau. The average cost of these expenses is fairly high. In those oblasts where circumcision is done openly and with full celebration of the ritual, the ceremony costs seven to eight thousand rubles. An "average" wedding costs about the same, not including the kalym. The dowry too costs about the same. Expenses for the dowry and for a gift to the groom can, in Asht Raion in Tajikistan, for example, reach 4,000 rubles (twenty bolts of cloth for the bride's dresses, at 150–170 rubles each, two suits, boots, a raincoat or overcoat for the husband-to-be, and a whole range of other things, often nonessential). The average cost of the dowry for most of Central Asia is around 6,000 rubles. This is accumulated over years, then spent, as rule, in the bazaars, where traders keep prices two to three times higher than in state stores. The bolts of cloth then lie in trunks, where over time their value falls significantly and sometimes even disappears. According to our calculations, in just one oblast, such as for example Andizhan Oblast, traders in such materials for the dowry can earn 120–130 million rubles a year.

It is impossible to accumulate such sums solely by economizing on food. Thus there are virtually no funds in the family budget for the intellectual development of the children. Visits to cultural events, other than infrequent trips to the cinema, are kept to a minimum, or even eliminated, for girls. There are virtually no children's books in rural households. Funds for the intellectual development of the parents are also insignificantly small. Even with such severe economizing, however, practice shows that the young married couple is unable to accumulate the sort of sums necessary for observing all the family rituals. Organizing the wedding and the circumcision for the first-born son is entirely the responsibility of the groom's parents. The father buys a wife for his son, entailing the kalym as well as payments for the wedding, and thus enslaves him. The son has to "work off" this "gift" from his father. Without the father's permission, the son cannot divorce his wife.

The kalym, the wedding, circumcision, and other such obligations tie the new family to the parents not just through debt but socially as well. If the father wishes it, the son will live separately; if he does not, the son will live in the father's home until the father dies. Until factual separation, the new family is neither economically nor socially an independent "unit of society." In the majority of agricultural regions of Central Asia, all married sons are formally regarded as having created independent families. As was already indicated, this is done to receive land allotments or, in livestock-breeding areas, to get the right to an independent herd. Public opinion, however, approves of and encourages undivided extended families, in which the possibility of controlling how the young people live is significantly higher. Division of the family is recognized only as an extreme measure. Land allotments provided for new households are devoted entirely to cash crops or to hay used as fodder for cash animals.

In recent years the students of Central Asian ethnography have noticed a rise in the number of so-called undivided families, or those in which the married sons live with the parents. Official statistics keep no records of this form of family; as far as government census figures go, the undivided family does not exist. It is easier and more profitable for undivided families to engage in petty commodity production, to concentrate the work force on plots belonging to or rented by one or another of the brothers. It is precisely the mercantile quality of the personal or family economy that is the main reason for not dividing the family.

Society condemns a son's departure from the family of his own accord. Only when he marries off his own son does a man separate his family "on a legal basis." This occurs when he is around forty and his son eighteen to twenty. Thus the departing son is soon to become a grandfather himself, which means he must attend the mosque, which will control his actions.

9

Traditional Child Rearing

> *Help ye one another in righteousness and piety, but help ye not one another in sin and rancour.*
>
> The Koran, V, 3

On the national level, the result of families saving for expenses connected with the observance of "national" rituals is obvious during the induction medical examinations at each call-up of the Soviet Army. Doctors find many young men to be in poor health, with certain diseases caused or conditioned by their life-style very common. Hernias are frequent, the result of heavy physical labor in childhood—labor that is wholly directed toward petty commodity production.

When our popular press raises the question of these rituals and customs (which it has only recently begun to do with any frequency), only the ethical side of these negative phenomena is considered—the moral cost. The main economic, or more precisely financial, side of so-called family rituals, which is where the money goes, is left out of the picture. Thus the criticism of these negative phenomena has no constructive consequences. Attempts to eliminate effects without first removing their initial causes can never be successful.

The situation of girls within the family deserves particular attention. The idea that a girl is "someone else's meat" continues to be strong even today. The girl's parents, or more often her father, think that in feeding and rearing a daughter the family is nurturing a worker for someone else's family, and so they must get as much good from the girl as they can during her stay in the parental home. The situation is particularly difficult for girls in Central Asian communities where the practice of payment of the kalym has been discontinued—that is, where there is no expected repayment for having fed her.

In practice, the work life of a girl begins at age six or seven when she begins to be taught all the skills of the female domestic sciences. Before marriage she must know how to bake bread, prepare food, sew clothing, clean the house and the courtyard, take care of the livestock, spin wool, flat-weave rugs, and much more. In the large families of Central Asia, a girl of seven may already be taking care of younger children. She is constantly bound to the home either because of having to care for younger brothers and sisters or because she is working at hard labor. It is not rare that a girl of ten will carry water in two large buckets (which is the norm for full-grown women in construction work), collect dried dung for fires, gather herbs, and so forth. In all this the girl gets almost no attention, even from her mother.

The situation of the boy in the family is significantly better. He enjoys the attention and concern of his parents because he is their future supporter and helper. His childhood is significantly more care-free than a girl's, at least in the early years.

The traditional upbringing of children in the Uzbek family was the subject of a special study based on the materials of our expedition. This study examines all aspects of education and behavior modification in the life of children within the family. Here I need draw attention only to what seems to be the main point.

In scholarly and popular literature, and sometimes in the newspapers, a great deal is said about the problems of child-rearing in Central Asian families, so this idea has become a fairly firm part of the common knowledge, not only among the native populations of Central Asia but among other peoples of our country as well.

Unfortunately, the opinion is far from true. Attentive study of this "child rearing" makes clear that it is nothing other than exploitation of child labor. It is possible to find any number of examples of parents fifty to fifty-five years old and younger living primarily on the labor of their under-aged children. It must undoubtedly be taken into account that large families require significant participation by the children in the family economy. At the same time, however, it is not possible to approve of the widely observed use of child labor in *public* economy, mostly picking cotton. In 1986 the participation of schoolchildren in the cotton harvest was severely restricted, so official accounts gave and continue to give an obviously false picture, one that minimizes their involvement.

The reaction of adults to my speeches before several different groups is very telling in this regard. Whenever I criticized the jobs given to children in the family economy as too difficult, I was always told that cotton picking was much worse. Not once in many years of such talks did anyone condemn the exploitation of children by their parents or criticize the adult male rural population, which takes practically no part (save for equipment drivers) in gathering cotton. The operative principle is that what is allowed for the family (or tradition) is not allowed for the state (or socialism).

The situation is particularly alarming in regions where tobacco is grown. The participation of children and of pregnant women in growing, harvesting, and processing this crop has a negative impact on the health of both, including genetic damage. In Moldavia, for example, the law forbids pregnant women and underage children from working with tobacco. In Central Asia, the republic rulers would seem to imply that the people belong to a different subspecies and so are not subject to the terrible effects of tobacco on their health.

Labor by girls is especially worthy of attention. Paradoxical though it may seem, labor by little girls has a direct effect on religious practice. Lifting and carrying heavy objects and undiagnosed childhood catarrhal diseases can lead to infertility. This is unequivocally confirmed by gynecologists, who note off the record that the official statistics understate female infertility in Central Asia.

In modern Central Asia an infertile woman is placed outside the law, for the inability to have children is considered the harshest possible "divine punishment." Women suffering from infertility rarely go immediately to a doctor. Usually at the onset of the condition they attempt "domestic remedies." The mullahs and the folk healers (known locally as the *znakhar*, the *bakhsh*, the *tabib*, and so forth), who use traditional folk medicines and methods, only make matters worse. The afflicted woman, at the recommendation and insistence of her family, and accompanied by an older woman and some relative of the husband, sets off for a *mazar*, a holy place. There, under the direction of a *sheik* (the guardian of the mazar), she undergoes some "secret cure," after which it often happens that even medical science is unable to help the infertile woman.

Such visits to mazars are not cheap. According to our calculations, not counting transportation costs, a visit to a "good" mazar costs a minimum of fifty rubles, and the "cure" always requires more than a single visit to the mazar. A client will generally visit a mazar at least two or three times for a single illness. The opinion current in scholarly literature that such visits to the mazar come solely at the initiative of the woman is untrue. Study of the question has shown that very often the initiative to visit the mazar comes from the husband of the infertile woman. It is thus incorrect to view the mazar as being only a "women's institution," as used to be the case.

Women turn to medical help only if all attempts at self-healing fail to give positive results. Here again, a complicated situation arises, for husbands very rarely will leave their wives in the hospital for the length of time necessary to cure the disease. Often they simply refuse to allow their wives to stay in the hospital at all.

Unsuccessful cures are followed by divorce. If she is lucky, the divorced woman's parents will still be able to work and to provide for her existence. Even today, there are many childless women in the villages who have no skills or jobs, and so cling to a marginal existence. Even in the houses of their fathers, such women live like poor relations. It can also happen that a husband will introduce a second wife into the home. When this occurs, the first marriage is not annulled, and the second one is Islamic, not registered in the proper state offices. Public opinion (in the mahalla) regards such situations as wholly normal.

In spite of all the efforts of the Soviet government, women continue to occupy a subservient position in Central Asian society. Two levels of female social status must be distinguished: the state and the familial. The first level offers women rights equal to those of men, while the second offers them none save the rights to work and to bear children. Rural women only rarely enjoy rights of the first level, and then only in the presence of some sort of government undertaking that provides jobs and allows them to realize the right to participate in the public economy. Only then does a woman get the chance for economic self-sufficiency, which is the necessary condition for social independence.

The differences in the situation of women in two villages of the Fergana valley, where this question was especially studied, are very instructive. The village of Varukh in the Isfara Raion and the village of Pangaz in the Asht Raion of Leninabad Oblast in Tajikistan are identical in natural, economic, and demographic conditions. In both, the primary sources of livelihood are fruit trees (apricots and apples) and livestock. Both villages are fairly large; Varukh has 16,000 people and Pangaz has 12,000. However, the position of women in the two is radically different.

In Varukh, a woman goes out on the street "in the Muslim manner," with all parts of her body carefully covered by clothing and her face covered by a kerchief. Girls of twelve and older do not go far from home alone and do not go to places of entertainment. When visiting anywhere, even within the village, they must have a chaperone, either an old woman or a male relative. Even answering a man's question on the street, to say nothing of conversing, is considered "unethical." In some homes in Varukh the wife of the master of the house will appear in the same room with male guests, but the rules of good behavior do not recommend that the wife go out on visits to nonrelatives. Girls and boys are never seen together outside of school.

Traditional Bride (village of Metk, Ganchin Raion, Tajikistan)

The picture in Pangaz is totally different. Women walk the streets freely, speak with people who ask them something, and they do not cover their faces. Teen-age boys and girls go about in the street together. In Pangaz, the majority of brides wear white dresses with European-style hats during the state wedding registration. The entire ritual is conducted in the European manner. A stage band of local schoolchildren plays. Of course, the *nikah,* or registration of the marriage by a mullah, is obligatory after the Soviet ritual; nevertheless, some dent has been made in the shari'a. That this is true is primarily due to the presence of a rug factory in Pangaz, where 130 women work; there is also a cottage-industry group of about 300 women who work at home, flat-weaving rugs. Even this small number of working women is enough to change the general situation for the better. Undoubtedly, Pangaz's close ties with the industrial city of Angren also play some role, since over the years some 500 families from

Modern Bride (Andijan Oblast, Uzbekistan).

Pangaz have been moved there. Such changes in the social status of women are even more visible in the village of Kuchkak, where many women work in an electronics factory in the settlement called KIM.*

On the other hand, there has also been a tendency in the ordinary family life of Pangaz that is generally viewed as negative—the recently observed growing number of divorces. Similar processes are also evident in the industrial regions of the Andijan Oblast of Uzbekistan. However, in this instance divorce can not be viewed as an entirely negative phenomenon. Divorce is also women's protest against the system of forced marriages and shows the growth of women's social activism, since the initiative for these divorces, excepting those for childlessness, comes from the "weaker sex." Divorce attests to the economic independence

---

*KIM is the Russian acronym for Communist Youth International.

of women. Unfortunately, though, it also attests to the preservation of old "national" customs in the family, so that we face a dialectic in which the progressive side (from our Soviet point of view) does not prevail. In particular, the dual social status of women is reflected in the dual nature of the economics of the family, where the state sector does not occupy the major position but is significantly inferior to family petty commodity production.

It is inarguable that participation in the state sector of the economy is of secondary importance for the greatest part of the rural Central Asian female population. This, in turn, leads to the exclusion of women from public life. It is precisely this circumstance that is the basic objective of traditionalism in all its hypostases.

The press and scholarly publications have devoted a great deal of attention to the subject of "Tradition and Women," while the reverse, "Women and Traditionalism," has scarcely been studied at all. There are several levels of relationships that must be delineated here. The first level is that of the little girl: all the attention she receives from adults has the object of teaching her how to observe the traditional norms of behavior. The second level is that of the teen-age girl. While still the object of adult attention, she herself is already teaching "good behavior" to those younger than she. The third level is that of the *kelin*, or young wife, whose mother-in-law demands that she observe all the norms and rules very strictly. When she has given birth to a few children, the woman will herself actively influence the young, demanding that they observe traditional norms of behavior. Finally, the ultimate keeper of traditional morals, the arbiter of norms of behavior and of rituals, is the mother-in-law, who is pitiless to household members in her demands for the observation of traditional prescriptions, a circumstance that must not be forgotten.

Thus, in the tradition that has evolved, the woman is the chief shaper of the next generation. By depriving this educator of a public life, traditionalism also deprives her of new information; in fact, it deprives her of any information that is not controlled by the traditional institutions of the village. The subject of the major role women play in the material education of children has been overlooked by theory and practice alike, but it is precisely here that we may find the foundation of all our mistakes, failures, and powerlessness, in atheistic and other propaganda.

Although the results of the expedition's investigations are reflected in the tables and charts in this book, when studying the mechanism of how religious information is transmitted to the next generation we deliberately placed religion at a disadvantage. This is because we deliberately excluded direct contacts between the children and religious institutions and clerics, such as the imams of the mosques, the sheiks of the mazars, and the *muallim* (teachers) in the underground *maktabs* (Muslim religious schools). In reality such contact occurs fairly regularly. However, even if there were no such contacts (which from the point of view of atheism would be ideal), religious affairs in the region under study would still be discouraging.

We studied how information is transmitted at the level of direct and constant contact between children and adults (Figure 2). We divided adults into two groups, those at home and those at school, and children were divided into two age and social groups, preschoolers and school-age children. Because of the specific nature of Central Asia (which is true of any region where the population professes Islam), boys and girls were examined separately. We found that the source of religious information is still the mosque and the mazar.

Table 6 (on page 70) shows the processes by which this information reaches children. These processes are invisible to traditional methods of study and thus have not yet been taken into account in either practical work or theoretical studies that apply to Central Asia. The first section of the table shows how information from various sources (in the given instance, educators) has identical significance for preschool and school-age boys. This is because a preschool boy gets information from the mosque through his grandfather. In short: *before he enters school, the boy is already a Muslim.* Remember that the mosque (meaning the mahalla) requires that a man begin to visit "the House of God" when he turns forty—that is, when a man becomes a grandfather.

68 TRADITIONALISM AND THE FAMILY

Figure 2. **Transmission of Religious Information**

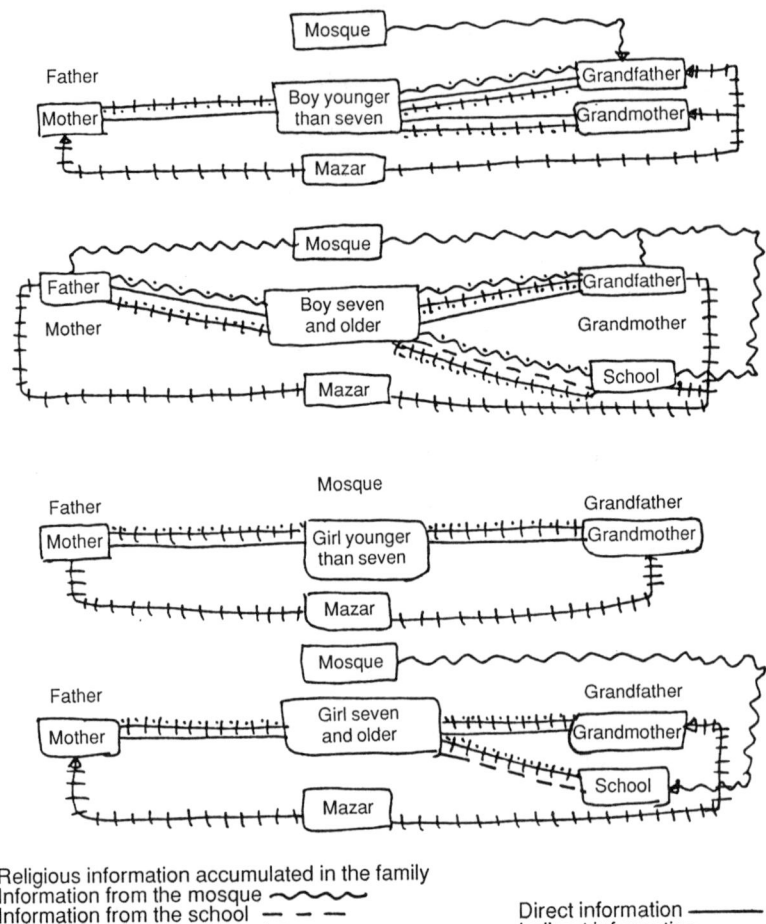

Religious information accumulated in the family
Information from the mosque ⌇⌇⌇
Information from the school — — —
Information from the mazar ┼┼┼┼

Direct information ─────
Indirect information • • • •

The grandfather is guided and controlled by the mosque in all aspects of his daily life, and he, in turn, educates and controls the behavior of his grandson. The circle remains closed. Both the mother (not to mention the mother-in-law), who is deprived of new information, and the grandfather, who filters new information through the prism of the mosque, are rearing an orthodox Muslim.

The table also identifies the social status of the person educating the child, revealing a wholly remarkable process in the educational system. Up until the age of seven, meaning until school age, religious information comes entirely from people who are not employed in the the public economy. As soon as the child goes off to school, he gets the lion's share of his information from people who work in public economy. This conclusion, which has been frequently confirmed, wholly contradicts the widespread but unproven idea that Islam in Central Asia is the territory and "zone of influence" of the least enlightened sectors of society— that is, those not connected with public production.

Unfortunately, in its various guises Islam is propagated by educated members of society. Naturally, it is hard to find a shepherd who would deny the divine revelations of Allah and Muhammad, separated as he is from society for many months while he follows his flocks. A much greater danger is presented by the rural teachers and doctors who cannot serve as models of atheism, even for schoolchildren, since they are themselves convinced Muslims. Such people may not conduct open religious propaganda in the schools and hospitals, but outside, their opinions and their example uphold Islam. Of course, it would be unjust to say this is true of all the teachers and doctors of rural Central Asia, who number among themselves some true materialists who are actively fighting against traditionalism. Their number, however, is not large, and they receive no support, so they cannot be said to predominate.

Scholarly pedagogical literature and the press constantly discuss the role of the family and the school in the shaping of the next generation, but traditionalism long ago resolved any prob-

Table 6

Transmission of Religious Information to Children (in weighted percentages; all information received = 100%)

	Transmitter of information										Source of information				
	employed in public economy							not employed in public economy Family			Outside school			Religious institutions	
	Family		School		Religious institutions		Total	Mosque	Mazar	Total	Religious institutions	Family	School	Mosque	Mazar
	Mosque	Mazar	Mosque	Mazar	Mosque	Mazar									
Boys younger than 7	—	—	—	—	—	—	—	67	33	100	29.4	70.6	—	67	33
7 and older	16.65	16.65	16.65	16.65	33.3	33.3	66.6	16.5	16.5	33.4	25.4	37.5	37.1	50	50
weighted avg. %	17.4	17.64	17.64	17.64	35.28	35.28	70.56	17.64	11.8	29.44	10.9	39.8	49.3	52.9	47.1
Girls younger than 7	—	—	—	—	—	—	—	—	100	100	20	80	—	—	100
7 and older	—	—	54.54	18.19	54.54	18.19	72.73	—	27.27	27.27	31.1	27.5	41.4	54.54	45.46
weighted avg. %	—	—	50	33.3	50	33.3	83.3	—	16.7	16.7	21.1	26.3	52.6	50	50

lems on this score. As may be seen from the figures in Table 6, the solution of the problem is differentiated according to sex and age. For boys up to age seven, two-thirds of the religious information comes from the mosque and one-third from the mazar. At school age, a third of the religious information that boys receive comes from the school.

As for girls, the picture is fundamentally different. Preschool girls are wholly "educated" by the mazar through contact with members of the family, while in the school years religious information from the mosque constitutes 54 percent and the share of the school almost 73 percent of all religious information. This paradox is easy to explain. In detailing the sources of information, it is plain that schoolboys are connected to the religious institutions through their families, while girls are connected through the schools. Why is this so? Because during their studies the boys have freedom of movement in their own mahalla and are able to visit with their fellow students, both in school and afterwards. They are able to take part in the social life of the mahalla at all times, even if passively for the time being.

Girls, especially those who have reached age twelve (marriageable age, according to the shari‘a, is *nine*), are deprived of the right to take free part in the activities of the mahalla. Until they marry, they may not keep even female company. The school remains the major and primary place where they encounter the outside world and get new information. In school, girls get three-fourths of their religious information from associating with their girlfriends, information that is strengthened by the elaborate institutional controls on girls' behavior. How schoolgirls observe "the rules of good behavior" is watched scrupulously by the school staff and the other female students. Any "mistake" a girl may commit is condemned by the mahalla and is inevitably punished.

The table also shows that in spite of the fact that a girl has no direct contact with the mosque, the mosque still supplies more than half of the religious information that a girl receives, a circumstance that surprised us.

It is clear that preschoolers receive religious information not only from their families but also, and to a significant degree, from direct contact with religious institutions. In fact, the share of this contact as a source of information is quite large, a little less than 30 percent for boys and 20 percent for girls.

During the school years, the proportion of information received directly from contact with religious institutions decreases for boys but increases for girls. In these years girls begin to visit the mazars. The figures also reflect the closer contacts some girls have with what in Tajik is called a *bibiotun* and in Uzbek an *otyncha*—the respective terms for a woman (deeply respected figures among the people) who oversees female ritual practices. At the same time, the figures in the table also reflect the separation of the boys (who by this time have already been circumcised) from the female part of the family, which makes their visits to the mazars more infrequent. Secondly, contact with the religious information flowing directly from religious institutions reaches boys through the mahalla and girls through school. This fact demands the closest possible attention and detailed study, based on the preparatory work that we have already done.

Finally, the table shows the significance of religious information coming from religious institutions. In general, the mosque is clearly more influential than the mazar, which could be due to the greater number of mosques than mazars, or might be a proof that mullahs have more influence than sheiks on the religious situation. It is also possible that both explanations are at work simultaneously.

This picture of how Islam prepares its adepts would be incomplete without an examination of the place religious information occupies in the general system of information that now exists in rural localities; this is presented in Table 7. The table divides the sources from which children receive information into six categories: religious institutions; family; mahalla and peers ("the street"); the mass media; school; and Soviet state organizations. This last category includes Komsomol, party, and government organizations.

CHILD-REARING 73

Table 7

Sources of Information for Children in Rural Areas (in percent)

	Boys		Girls	
Source of information	under 7	7 and older	under 7	7 and older
Uncontrolled				
Religious institutions				
Mosque	2.5	2.46	3.8	2.0
Maktab	—	3.85	—	—
Mazar	4.2	3.85	11.5	8.0
Bibiotun	12.75	1.54	6.2	4.0
	19.45	*13.7*	*21.5*	*14.0*
The Family				
Grandfather	6.3	6.55	9.3	2.46
Grandmother	6.3	2.18	4.7	3.78
Father	6.3	6.55	9.3	1.89
Mother	3.1	3.27	4.7	2.46
	22.0	*18.55*	*28.0*	*10.6*
"The street"				
Peers	2.1	5.29	3.2	7.1
Mahalla	6.3	4.0	13.2	14.2
	8.4	*9.29*	*16.4*	*21.3*
Total	49.85	41.54	65.9	45.9
Controlled				
Mass media				
Movies	4.2	2.78	2.8	4.37
Television	12.75	2.78	2.8	1.45
Radio	12.75	2.78	2.8	1.45
Newspapers	2.1	2.78	2.8	1.45
Books	2.5	2.78	2.2	4.37
	34.3	*13.9*	*13.4*	*13.1*
School				
Teacher	—	10.88	—	10.9
Student circle	—	10.88	—	10.9
Pioneers	—	10.88	—	10.9
	—	*32.64*	—	*32.7*
State organs				
Komsomol	—	6.18	—	1.82
Communist party	3.1	1.54	5.2	1.82
Soviet organs	12.75	6.18	15.9	4.55
	15.65	*13.9*	*21.1*	*8.2*
Total	50.15	58.46	34.1	54.1

The six categories comprise two groups. The first, containing religious institutions, the family, and the "street," represents information not controlled by the government; the second group—mass media, school, and Soviet state organizations—carries information that must at least pass through government control.

The category for religious institutions is subdivided into four sources, the two from the previous table and two new ones. The first of these is the maktab, the underground religious school, which can and does have various functional forms. Usually the instruction is individual: a "literate mullah," meaning a man who knows Arabic, teaches the language to a boy, using the Koran as the primary text of instruction. According to our observations, group lessons occur much more infrequently; this does not mean that such groups are few in number, but rather that individual study is even more common. At almost every educational level there is at least one student who is studying at a maktab. As student bodies are defined on territorial lines, the Muslim clergy are thus educating a cleric for a defined territory—namely, their mahalla. This means that the future shepherd knows his flock from childhood, just as the flock knows its future leader. No secret is made of this study of "the Arabic language," which is "a good thing."

The second new source of information is the woman whose function bears different names in different parts of Central Asia—*bibiotun, otyncha, folbin,* and others. Her role might with some stretching be compared with the activity of the mullahs of the underground maktabs. The bibiotun is the arbiter of all female functions, which means that she regulates all ritual practices prescribed solely for women. The bibiotun has one or two pupils (rarely three) whom she teaches "proper behavior," which makes her the conduit of traditions between the generations.

As this table shows, the "street" is an important and significant source of information. The "street" has two constituent parts, the peer group and the mahalla. The role of peers—that is, the child's cohort—as a source of information for every child has been reasonably well elaborated by pedagogues, psychologists, and sociologists. I would note only that the nature of this information is primarily determined by very concrete, immediate situations, which could be encompassed by the influence of the family, where the practice of "immediate" actions especially flourishes. The role of the mahalla in the transmission of information has not been well researched. The mahalla has mostly been studied as a structural phenomenon of the Central Asian city, or in connection with settlement patterns among craftsmen or the tax units of a city. The religious functions of neighborhood mosques have been noted, but as a social mechanism that regulates and regenerates its particular way of life, the mahalla has remained untouched. Moreover, there is virtually no information whatever about the rural mahalla.

The nature of this work does not permit a complete examination of the full variety of mahalla activities, so I will only delineate the basic tendencies and set out the main conclusions that have emerged in the study of this topic so far.

10

The Mahalla

> *God doth command . . . when ye judge between man and man, that ye judge with justice.*   The Koran, IV, 58

The neighborhood mahalla is a transformation of the traditional Central Asian society of neighbors, adapted for modern social and economic conditions. This is true in both the city and the countryside. The history of the mahalla goes back to the extended family grouping of the Tajik avlod. In mountainous villages these labor groupings existed right up until the 1930s and 1940s. Men of seventy and eighty still remember the structure of such groups, made up of extended families. Transformation of the avlod into the mahalla proceeded faster in the city. Both institutions coexisted for a long time, until the mahalla eventually prevailed in economic and social life, leaving the avlod to function solely as a kinship group.

   With the introduction of Soviet rule, and the nationalization of both land and the means of production, the economic basis for the mahalla was eliminated in the city. In the countryside, however, it only changed form. The differences between the modern mahalla and that of the past (the 1900s–1920s) are obvious. As capitalism destroyed traditional craft production, the urban mahalla began to break down. The beginning of Soviet rule stopped this process, and during the chaotic early postrevolutionary years, craftsmen provided people with the goods they needed through the marketplace. The social structure of the mahalla also stabilized, greatly assisted by mahalla ownership of the irrigation systems, which were vital to Central Asian cities even thirty years ago. Preservation of the mahalla within the cities generally led to the mahalla becoming the social unit of the city in the Soviet period as well.

Official Soviet recognition of the electoral commission of the mahalla as a controlling body not only established the mahalla in an organizational way as the constituent unit of the modern city but also legalized its functions, the majority of which are not sanctioned for this type of urban organism. Legalizing the mahalla not only meant preserving the structure in the old parts of the city, but also meant recreating it in the new areas of high-rise apartment buildings. Architects, scholars, and publicists discuss the plans for modern buildings in the pages of scholarly and popular journals, to determine which have created the best conditions for neighborly contact. No doubt it would be stupid to protest against neighborly contact, but such contact conceals one of our most dangerous social landmines, which is especially powerful in small Central Asian cities and urbanized villages. Practice shows that resettlement in new apartment buildings often proceeds by mahalla. Sometimes an entire street settles into one new building, and the neighboring buildings are settled by people from the same mahalla. One should recall that in addition to being a productive and territorial unit, the mahalla has also always been a religious and organizational unit, forming a parish, or *kaum*. As has been noted, even in the underground maktabs the mullahs organize classes by mahalla, so that the structure is always preserved.

As for the neighborhood committees, the way in which they are elected (as for example in the Fergana valley) seems scandalous at the very least. In the vast majority of instances the committee members are appointed by the elders of the mahalla, with representatives of the regional soviet or the city soviet attending. Women are very rarely chosen for these committees. The committee of the mahalla regulates the entire social and personal life of its territory. It shapes public opinion, policing observation of norms of behavior derived from shari'a, adat, and local practices that are noncanonical but obligatory. Any violation of the mahalla's way of doing things is inescapably followed by punishment in the form of social censure and shunning of the violator's home by the other residents, including not inviting that individual to *toi* (religious celebrations) organized by the mahalla. Should the rebellious resident leave the mahalla, his "bad reputation" will follow him. Even selling a private house is impossible without the consent and approval of the mahalla. If the committee members (or elders) do not approve of the buyer, then no sale will take place. Should the deal go through in spite of the committee's opinion, then the new owner of the house will be put in such a predicament that he will move again of his own accord.

In addition to regulating the "demographic situation," the mahalla also has ideological life entirely and firmly in its hands. The committee and its active members, the elders, use very refined techniques to direct the education of youth. The channeling and, even more important, the interpretation of information is extremely simple: the forty-year-old father passes it from the mosque to his twenty-year-old son and his year-old grandson. It is noteworthy that in many settlements (for example in Namangan Oblast) mahalla committee buildings substitute for mosques and in fact are built on the sites of old religious buildings. Collective Friday prayers are not a rarity in these buildings.

The mahalla keeps very close track of the way in which women observe the norms of behavior. Essentially the committee works in close contact with the mullah, the bibiotun, and the sheik (which is the name given in most of the regions of Central Asia to the man who is responsible for a mazar and who regulates ritual practice; often the job of sheik is passed from father to son). It can also happen that all three people are on the committee itself. In rural localities there is not even a pretense that the mahalla committee is elected. After all, the rural mahalla has been preserved because it has a real economic basis even today, in the local irrigation system and the collective labor required to clean and maintain it. In rural areas the mahalla controls all aspects of life for people, including information transmission, even more completely than it does in cities.

For boys, the information that is not under government control, including that which comes from the "street" (the mahalla), is noticeably reduced after a boy starts school, and is replaced by the information received in school. This process is extremely important for understanding the mechanism of information transmission in general and of the education of a Muslim in particular. The child is already a Muslim when he begins school, for the mahalla has already finished its work. At school age all that goes on is the "polishing" and "touching up" of details. The mahalla is concerned only with observing the most necessary behavioral norms, which it corrects through the father.

The process proceeds in another way for girls. It is important here to note the greater influence that the mosque and family have for girls in the preschool years, relative to boys. The mahalla (or "street") remains in the background, but in spite of its low quantity, the significance (weight) of such information is paramount. The mahalla does not ignore the future shaper of the next generation. Information from state organs and mass media could have, or more exactly, should have considerably more significance for preschool girls. This could occur if there were active councils of women. Such influence appears in Table 7 as information coming from the Komsomol, but this supposes the existence of kindergartens and other preschool institutions, all of which are almost nonexistent in rural Central Asia. The table treats this factor as though it were actually functioning, or had some effect, even though in reality it has none, in order to demonstrate the progressive significance it could have. Our considerable successes in the restructuring of Central Asian society during the 1930s were in large part made possible by the active work of women's councils and the Komsomol.

Particular attention should be paid to the role of religious institutions in the column for girls (Table 7). Although they have no direct contact with it, girls still receive a great deal of their information from the mosque, which forces us to examine a connection that previously was supposed not to exist, that between women and the mosque. To assume that women have contact only with the mazar is a serious mistake. The idea that women have no part in the mosque is actively advanced both by the scholarly literature on atheism and by the clergy. While the clergy's reasons for saying so are wholly understandable, the incompetence of the scholars simply works to the benefit of Islam. The prohibition against women attending the mosque in no way means that the imam pays them no attention; in fact, the findings of our expedition indicate that the direct opposite is true. Scholarly ignorance of processes going on in society does not mean that they do not exist.

Tradition precisely regulates norms of behavior by age. Pre–school-age children are taught unquestioning obedience of their elders, although here too there is a significant difference between boys and girls. A boy is permitted a great deal, while a girl is permitted nothing, meaning that she is trained to suppress any manifestation of youthful emotions. However, in spite of these differences in upbringing, near the end of middle school the situations for both girls and boys have become similar in many ways, since the elders of both try to control everything they do, the only difference being the severity of the prohibitions. However, once they have finished school, meaning essentially once they have come of age, boys and girls find that their respective conditions and methods of education diverge sharply. Once a young man has finished army duty or completed a course at an institute of higher learning, many of the prohibitions are lifted (nor is it uncommon to have them lifted while he is still at the institute). However, young women, who by this time have become wives and mothers, find that prohibitions grow even more absolute; compare this with the growth in significance of information that schoolgirls receive from the mahalla. It is here that we see most fully the mother-in-law's role as bearer and transmitter of traditional ways.

11

Gender and Behavior

O mankind! your insolence is against your own souls!
The Koran, X, 23

A young man's freedom of behavior is restricted only within a traditional environment, and constraints grow weaker the farther the young man gets from his mahalla (or the high-rise apartment building that is its analogue). When a young man is at home, public opinion very strictly regulates his behavior, but away from this environment there are no such restraints. The young man is also reared to neither respect nor obey nontraditionalist standards of behavior. The consequences may be seen in the events that occurred in Alma-Ata in 1986, in Fergana in 1989, and in Baku and Sumgait.*

It is no accident that the main actors in these events were young men. The much-acclaimed idea of respect for one's elders may serve to confirm that behavior is chosen according to surroundings, since observations from various parts of Central Asia and other regions of the USSR attest uniformly that such behavior is selective. The nearer he is to his home and the greater the number of other Muslims immediately about him, the greater the

---

*Poliakov is referring to the antigovernment riots that followed the dismissal of Kazakhstan's Communist party first secretary, D.A. Kunaev, and his replacement by a Russian, in December 1986; fighting between Uzbeks and Meskhet Turks in the Fergana valley in Uzbekistan; and the conflict between Azerbaijanis and the Armenian minority in Azerbaijan.

respect the Muslim shows for his elders. However, behavior is even more selective, in that greater respect is given to other fellow-believers than to non-Muslims. This becomes quite open in Moscow, where being in a non-Muslim environment completely deprives the Muslim of his supposedly in-born sense of deference to old age and he shows no more respect than does any other, non-Muslim group of the population. It is worth noting that the only positive reason traditionalists offer to defend the preservation and development of traditional norms is this idea of "respect for elders." In fact, most useful standards of behavior have been lost, and new ones have not taken their place.

A large part of traditionalist education is learning a system of comparing Soviet law and the shari'a on the everyday level. Those points of Soviet law that do not openly contradict shari'a law are observed fairly rigorously. But such norms are few in number. The consequence is massive violation of Soviet law (an example already given is laws about land use). Producing income in any way possible and refusing to admit the existence of public property have become standard behavior, sanctioned by tradition. A successful "merchant" (in other words, a swindler) achieves society's recognition. The only thing that is not condoned is stealing in one's immediate environs. Theft in the government sector is not considered shameful, nor is dirty-dealing in trade, whether with the state or at the bazaar, although these are as much violations of the ethical norms of both shari'a and adat as they are of Soviet law.

Once a man has reached forty, anarchic behavior is not condoned. Attendance at the mosque becomes obligatory, as does payment of the religious tax, atonement for the sins of youth, and the education of grandchildren and children in the traditionalist spirit. In addition to this last obligation, "behavioral traditionalism" among men is also attributable to the fact that by the time a man has reached forty his family becomes economically and socially independent. Once he has married off his son or become a grandfather, a man has the right to separate and create his own "nuclear" family. This has been noted during years of observations throughout Central Asia and confirmed many times over. Such confirmation is important, because it reveals the economic foundation of traditionalism in everyday life. This sort of traditionalism requires economically independent people and will not function without them. The expedition's materials uniformly attest that families that exist solely on their legal income and have no large material surpluses are less interested in traditionalism. I would note that their expenditures for "national" rituals are also comparatively small and that observance of such rituals is not as zealous as in those families in which there are "men of respect."

The system of transmission of religious information (Table 6) should be recalled here, since children get a large part of this information from people who work in the state sector, which means they are economically independent. The great majority of these are men. Women achieve financial independence only in the very rarest of instances, and only where there is some form of industry, either in the village itself or nearby.

The standards of behavior for married women are best defined by the postulate that "a good woman is silent and never leaves home without her husband." The contemporary position of women in the family as it is presented in ethnographic scholarship about Central Asia is far from the real truth. The widely held notions about how women "used to be" downtrodden, without rights or remedy, do not reflect the full complexity and contradiction of the real situation, which has a great many nuances, with both regional and social aspects.

Girls are commonly taught complete obedience to the will of their parents, replaced after marriage by obedience to their husbands. Despite all the difficulties a newlywed young woman encounters in the family of her husband, girls are nevertheless eager to marry and leave the home. This is caused by more than a simple feeling that "it is time to become a mother." Freedom of action is a psychological factor of equal importance; in her own family a girl is considered a useless appendage, and is denied many, if not all, the pleasures of being a young person. The materials that the expedition has gathered over the past ten years show that an important factor in a girl's willingness to marry even a boy whom she does not know is the opportunity marriage gives her to wear a new dress, to adorn herself, to try on all the clothes she gets as her dowry. It makes no difference here whether the young woman is able to go outside of her new home, which is very rare, or whether she stays at home; she gets equal satisfaction from both.

Most women also like their position in the family, which might be described as "unthinking." As long as the young couple lives with the boy's parents, the bride does not have to make decisions about anything, because her husband and her mother-in-law tell her what to do. According to the traditions of the mahalla, the husband has full "official" responsibility for providing the family with its needs—groceries, clothing, fuel, and so forth—while the wife is only responsible for how these products are used within the home. Even the quantity of something, let us say groceries, that the husband brings home does not always reveal the family's real material situation. It is not uncommon for a husband to supply his family at a minimum level, and sometimes even lower, while also having large savings. This is called a "frugal" way of life. In these cases the wife will work on the side, if she knows a craft; sometimes her earnings will contribute significantly to the family budget, but that does not change her social status within the family. Even today the custom (or rule) of "separate purses" for husband and wife is widely observed. Often a woman does not spend the money she earns on family needs, but uses it to buy things only for herself. As a rule this occurs in those families in which the mother-in-law is not very powerful or where the young couple lives alone.

Relations between spouses are rarely confiding or close. More often husband and wife seem to be a partnership for the production and rearing of children. According to the prevalent standards of behavior, spouses must conceal their mutual affection (if it exists) even from their own children.

Traditional norms for family life are so strong that a woman has no need to register her marriage at the state registry office, unless she wishes to be classified as a "self-employed worker." The *nikah,* or marriage by the Muslim rituals defined by shari'a law, is sufficient. Public (mahalla) opinion does not condemn a woman in such a marriage even if she is the second or third wife and only the first is registered according to Soviet law. She is regarded as a lawful wife, with all the rights and duties. The great majority of women make no open protest against this practice; divorces and other forms of protest are provoked by wife beating or by psychological oppression on the part of the husband's relatives, especially the mother-in-law and sisters-in-law.

The most common form of protest is that the bride returns to her parents' house. As a rule, this act does not produce positive results for a woman. Often the bride's parents themselves force her to return to the house of her husband, and the mahalla exacts cruel revenge for her independence.

In contemporary rural conditions it is extremely complicated for a woman to get a divorce, if she is the initiator. However, a man can get a divorce very easily; he is considered free after repeating three times the word *talak* (Arabic for "divorce"). Nor is it necessary to register the divorce in the Soviet registry offices, since everyone in the village will know that he is no longer married.

The act of despair to which women turn today is suicide. The usual methods are self-immolation and poisoning—most commonly by drinking vinegar essence. The only time any official record is made of such attempts is when there are legal consequences; there is no record of the number of women whose attempts are unsuccessful. Even so, unfortunately, the number of such tragedies is still high. Moreover, public opinion condemns only the "thoughtlessness" and "immorality" of the woman who has killed herself, and not the people who drove her to her death. The primary issue in such cases is the determined struggle to quash any attempt to blame such tragedies on traditionalism. All of the "respectable" people and the mahalla rise to defend tradition, to portray it as blameless. Frequently the intelligentsia takes an active part in this defense.

Equally astonishing is how the female part of rural society views such acts. Very few women sympathize with their sisters who have been driven to suicide, and the vast majority condemn such a suicide roundly. The mahalla plays the leading role here too, as may clearly be seen in Table 7. After a girl finishes school, the share of information that came from school is replaced by information from the mahalla, which after marriage also replaces the portion she was getting from the mass media. In the best of circumstances a married woman may retain this latter source of information in the very truncated form of television and radio. This is the case for almost all girls. For example, in 1986 about 750 girls completed middle school in Asht Raion of Leninabad Oblast. Only 35 of these went on to higher education, while the rest, more than 700 of them, fell into the hands of mothers-in-law and the mahalla, the bibiotun, and the mosque. There too, just as with the young men, everything returns to its usual orbit.

To conclude discussion of how children are educated, it should be noted (in Table 7) that information not under government control predominates for girls of preschool age, whereas for boys, uncontrolled and controlled information are essentially about equal. What this means is that the part of society that will primarily nourish and shape the succeeding generation is also the part for whom traditionalist ways predominate.

12

The Family Budget

> *And do not eat up your property among yourselves for vanities.*
> The Koran, II, 184

The items of the family budget are an important indicator of the condition of modern Central Asian society, but the study of this question is far from what it should be. To date Soviet scholars who have studied this question have only been able to impose very broad formal typological groupings and have yet to quantify spending categories. Our methodology needs to be improved, since the data obtained from questionnaires and gathered by observation show a very wide deviation in the absolute cost claimed for various undertakings.

We divide the whole family budget into two groups of expenses—rational and nonrational. Of course this division does not reflect the point of view of a Central Asian Muslim. It is also to a certain degree conditional, since it is one of our working hypotheses and models of investigation. Between these two groups is the category of expenses for the "private economy." From the viewpoint of petty commodity production these expenses are "rational," while from the standpoint of socialism they are unquestionably "nonrational."

We describe each expense as being one of three possible types: "fully met" (denoted by a plus sign); "not fully met" (a minus sign), and "varies situationally" (plus/minus). The preliminary nature of such ranking is obvious, but it does allow for very

Figure 3. **The Rural Family Budget**

Key: + = fully met; − = not full met; ± = varies situationally

RATIONAL EXPENDITURES

on private economy:

upkeep of agricultural plot +
upkeep of livestock +
land cultivation, harvesting +
sale of produce +
payment for pasturage +

for personal use:

food −
clothing −
housing +
durable goods +
motor transport +
intellectual development
  of family members −
education −

NONRATIONAL EXPENDITURES

on Islamic holidays:

mosque +
uraz bairam +
kurban bairam +

on family rituals:

"child's cycle" +
circumcisions +
weddings +
burials +
memorial banquets +
required festivals +

on mahalla needs:

upkeep of the neighbor-
  hood committee +
neighborhood celebrations +
upkeep of cultural facilities
  (buildings, mazars, etc.) +

Income: private economy and wages from kolkhoz or sovkhoz

Accumulated wealth: cattle, land, gold and valuables, cash

general conclusions about the necessity of expenditures for one or another item of the family budget, and about the degree to which the demands of tradition must be satisfied. "Rational" expenditures, those for the family, are also ranked according to the same three categories: met, not met, and variably met.

In the case of the private economy, needs are always met sufficiently, sparing no expense.

There is also no scrimping with so-called social necessities. In essence this involves meeting the demands of the mahalla for keeping "national traditions," which simply means observing traditional rituals and supporting the clergy. In general 62 percent of the budget items are met, 24.3 percent are variably met, and 13.7 percent are not met.

As for budget items paid for from "savings," meaning from

accumulated wealth, here too the nonrational predominates. Expenditures for "valuables," for example, "vary situationally," which means that there is no obligation to fund them, but also indicates that often a part of savings cannot be rationally employed. This situation demands very close attention, since this is the "financial environment" in which children are reared, and so is a living preview of their future behavior. Certainly for the young men (20 to 25 years old) from whom we gathered our materials, the family budget was distributed along the lines of the system outlined in Figure 3. It is true that they were delaying full observation of the "national rituals" until they had achieved the age of their fathers, meaning full economic independence for their own families. This is also the age at which men complete their course of study in the received wisdom of the rural economy.

This schematization is the family budget. For now most of the items can only be described as "met," "not met," and "met as circumstances permit." At present we can make more concrete description of expenditures only for ritual practices. We may cite as an example a region of Osh Oblast, in Kyrgyzstan, with the caveat that the amounts spent on ritual practices are quoted at their lowest possible cost (the data on such costs were obtained by our questionnaire).

In 1988 the population of this region was about 57,000, and the combined income was 16,445,000 rubles. Pensions amounted to 302,000 rubles, so that in toto the population was paid 16,747,000 rubles (excluding subsidies for large families). According to official figures (supplied by the executive committee of the regional soviet), that year in the region:

- there were 503 weddings, each with an average cost of 10,000 rubles, meaning that 5,030,000 rubles were spent;
- 1,300 boys were born and a somewhat larger number attained age 7, meaning that on the average 1,300 circumcisions were performed, each costing 4,000 rubles, for a total expenditure of 5,200,000 rubles;
- 200 adults died, their funerals cost 1,000 rubles each, for total

expenditures of 200,000 rubles, with the same number of memorial celebrations for another 200,000 rubles;
- the rituals of the "child's cycle" (celebrations marking the birth and naming of a child) cost 6,500 families 100 rubles each, meaning 650,000 rubles.

The total expenditure for all these ritual observances was 11,280,000 rubles. That left 5,467,000 rubles of income drawn from the government payroll and pensions. Simple division of 5,467,000 rubles by 57,000 residents gives 96 rubles a year, which divided by 365 means less than 30 kopeks per day per person to meet all other living expenses. Obviously it is wholly impossible to live on so little money, which leads to the conclusion that 70 percent of the population must live on the private economy, as was discussed in detail above. This also makes the connection between traditionalism and the petty commodity economy very clear.

Traditionalist ritualism (which people often attempt to describe as "traditions of the people") requires enormous sums. Above we cite only the minimum costs; in reality the costs are generally a good deal higher. Nor do the figures above include money to support the mosques and holy places or the mahalla committees, or to celebrate such traditional Islamic holidays as *kurban-bairam,* (the feast of Ibrahim) and *uraz-bairam* (marking the end of the Ramadan fast).

At this point we should return to discussion of the phase of "anarchic behavior" which comes after a young man has completed school and is away from native environs. In fact this only appears to be untrammeled behavior, because what occurs during this period is that the young man learns about the outside world and gets practical experience for serious business undertakings outside of his native society. In the rural areas there are almost no men over thirty who have not gone "with caravans of goods into foreign lands." If a man has little of his own to sell, then he is given goods by his father or by one of his close relatives, and the profit is split, depending upon how hard the seller works. In trade and in other business the middleman must always be paid. This incidentally is the source of the "legality" of bribery and of payment for conveying the bribe; both are considered to have been earned.

To conclude the examination of how each new generation is educated, it must be stressed that no "youth problem" exists in Central Asia. Young people are always controllable. The few rebels who try to change their way of life are forced either to leave Central Asia or, what is far more common, to submit, as I have seen myself, in the case of one of the most talented young people I have ever met. I knew him both as schoolboy and as graduate student, and found that his cultivation and erudition could be envied by people much older and better educated. Even though he was from a family of intellectuals, his attempts to change the existing order not only were very quickly quashed but were quashed with the help of one of his relatives who was an important person in the republic.

In addition to giving a young man a traditionalist education, the system teaches him to reject everything that contradicts traditionalism. This is one of the greatest sources of traditional society's resilience: that the Soviet system is forced to try to reeducate someone who is already an idealist rather than simply educate someone to be a materialist. Practice suggests that Soviet efforts here have so far been in vain.

Islam devotes very little time to education by the word. The primary burden of education is borne by example and by action, with words used only to comment on actions and behavior. In this regard the system of prohibition is interesting. It is never explained why some act or other is prohibited; it is simply forbidden. Someone who has broken a rule expects to be punished not because of something concrete that he has done, but because he has violated a prohibition. Words are to explain and annotate this for the other children and young men, which reinforces unthinking submission to tradition and "the elders." The entire system of submission is built on the fear of punishment, irrespective of who administers it.

An extraordinarily important part of the system of traditional education is the preservation and praise of the experience of previous generations. Experience is never discredited. The mechanism of its transmission is extremely simple; you are to do as your elders did. This constitutes the entire meaning of so-called labor education. Boys and girls of ten to twelve years of age (and sometimes even younger) are shown and forced to copy precisely what their elders do, whether in a craft, in household chores, or in behavior. The elder is always an authority, which is why Central Asia does not have the problems with the elderly that have grown so acute in many industrial countries. The older person is always a teacher and his authority is unquestionable, which also means that old people are upholders of tradition, the mosque, and the whole complex of the mahalla. The circle is again closed. Absolute respect for elders becomes an impediment to progress, just as any sensible idea, raised to an absolute, becomes its opposite, or absurd.

IV

THE ROLE OF RELIGION IN THE COMMUNITY

13

Religious Institutions

> *Nor dost thou ever pray for any of them that dies, nor stand at his grave.*   The Koran, IX, 84

At present the only Muslim religious institutions in Central Asia that function officially are a *medresseh* (seminary) in Bukhara, a religious academy in Tashkent, and registered mosques, the total number of which is not large.* For example, in Leninabad Oblast of Tajikistan there are three mosques, two in the oblast capital and one in the regional center of Proletarsk. Essentially the same picture obtains in the majority of regions of Central Asia. But official statistics are deceptive; unfortunately they are far from a reflection of the real state of affairs.

Shaped by the family, with the aid of the mahalla, the male Muslim falls directly into the lap of the mosque, while the female Muslim falls into the hands of the sheiks of the mazar and the bibiotun (or otyncha). The number of officially registered religious institutions does not constitute even one percent of the mosques and mazars that actually operate and that regulate the Muslim's way of life, defining his ideology.

Official mosques only represent "government Islam." "Everyday Islam" has vastly more religious institutions at its disposal.

---

*Poliakov's enumeration of the existing religious institutions was accurate when he completed his manuscript in December 1989. Since then, however, hundreds of new mosques have been opened, as have a number of medresseh, including a fundamentalist-oriented medresseh in Dushanbe.

When the expedition was in northern Tajikistan (which includes the western part of the Fergana valley) we found more than 200 functioning mosques, and over the entire span of the expedition's work we have found more than 400. Each kishlak, or village, has a minimum of one mosque, and in some villages each mahalla has its own "house of God." For example, in the kishlak of Varukh in the Isfara Raion of Tajikistan, the number of functioning underground mosques is roughly equal to the number that existed at the time of the Kokand khanate. We have recently found archival documents that give the number of mosques in some kishlaks of northern Tajikistan before the establishment of Soviet rule. Comparison with today shows that there are no fewer now, and in some settlements there are more because as the population has grown, so too has the number of mosques.

The buildings of the old mosques continue to be used and are kept up by the inhabitants of the village themselves. The most important maintenance work is what it always was, keeping the roof repaired; because it is made of clay it is the weakest part of the building. This apparently insignificant detail is very telling, because there has been an extremely severe shortage of roofing tiles in Central Asia for at least ten years, but there are always some to be found for roofing the mosque. Another point deserves mention as well: that building materials intended for construction of a religious edifice can lie around unguarded anywhere in Central Asia and no one will touch them, which cannot be said of either state or private construction materials.

In recent years the maintenance of the old mosques was halted for a period, primarily because local organs of power were held more strictly accountable for observation of the laws restricting religious observance (though this was not uniformly enforced), but also because cosmetic or minor repair of old mosques was no longer enough to save buildings that were in disastrous condition. An uninitiated observer might then conclude that such mosques are abandoned and nonfunctioning. In some instances this is the case, but the majority of places where mosques are located are used by the rural inhabitants to practice their religion. If the building of a mosque is in danger of collapse for whatever reason, the canons of Islam forbid praying in it, so in such situations a *hujra,* a structure with light and heat, is erected on the grounds of the mosque, alongside the old building. Originally such buildings, which are part of the grounds of a mosque or mazar, were probably where Sufi sheiks lived and taught, but following the (illegal) closure of mosques in Central Asia, the hujra itself assumed the function of the mosque.

We may assume that when it is absolutely necessary, hujras are built on the private plots of village residents. This tactic is particularly common in new settlements, where there are no old "holy" plots of land. Whoever owns the land allotment becomes the imam of this new mosque. The official explanation for such a building is that it is used for gatherings of the "elders" (men over forty), where they may "discuss their affairs." In fact this is a new mosque, with the sole difference that the architecture is entirely "civilian." Furthermore, it is argued that praying in such buildings is "canonical," because the first mosque was simply the Prophet's house; even in this instance Islam justifies the actions of its adherents. In recent years this practice has grown less frequent because a greater number of hujras and mosques have been "reopened" in the villages after being wholly rebuilt.

The attitude of the Central Asian population to nonfunctioning mosque buildings is quite indifferent. Many such structures contain warehouses, stores, and so on, although it is also true that recently the situation has begun to change somewhat. For example, in the village of Pangaz one of the salespeople in a store that was housed in a former mosque began to complain of illnesses caused by the spirits who still dwell in the mosque, which the people who live near the store readily affirm. Investigators often explain such phenomena as a "god-fearing" reaction to the building, from which they conclude that the buildings of the mosque as such are held in reverence. Although such reverence for the structure of a mosque may exist, materials gathered by the expedition strongly suggest another conclusion: that the building is respected only when services are held within it, meaning that the mosque is a functioning one. The greatest respect is accorded to the buildings of mosques located on cemeteries or next to some sort of burial ground, regardless of whether the mosque is functioning or not. But in that case it is the holiness of the burial ground that is transferred to all the buildings on the site; the building itself is not considered holy and can be partially destroyed for utilitarian reasons—for example, if more space is needed to build housing (as happened in the settlement of Unji in Leninabad Oblast, Tajikistan).

However, it is true that in some places, Dushanbe for example, the mosque is becoming a symbol for holiness in general. Thus laborers at a Dushanbe jewelry factory that was built on the site of a mosque argue that the main explanation of the factory's disorganization and their failure to meet production goals is the factory's site. The most likely explanation for this attitude toward the sites of former mosques is the scarcity of "holy places" in a modern industrial city. There is no such shortage in rural locales, and so mosques are respected according to their "utility"—whether they are used for group prayer.

This essentially disrespectful attitude toward the building of a mosque speaks of the building's "nonsanctity." Sanctity, as has been noted, is conferred only by the prayers offered in the building. By and large the mosque was regarded in the past to be a place provided by the government, and in today's conditions as a place provided by the public, where the male population of the mahalla or village may gather. When passing by the former building of a nonfunctioning mosque many Muslims fail to make an *omin*. As recently as ten or fifteen years ago many mosques also still had *osh-khona* and *alou-khona*, places that not only are not connected with orthodox Islam but are directly antithetical to it. The osh-khona is a place for eating (*osh*: food, a meal; and *khona*: a room or building), and the alou-khona is the fire-house or fire-temple among the Zoroastrians. These were places where the men gathered for collective meals and where they kindled the holy fire. The degree to which such places still exist today requires more study, because the situation is constantly changing.

Whatever the case, it is certainly true that the big cauldrons in which food is prepared during holidays, as well as the other holiday vessels that are the common property of the mahalla, are all kept in the mosques. Hearths at which food is prepared are common in the courtyards of mosques even today, and the explanation that they are for heating water for ritual ablutions is not satisfactory, since such hearths have fresh ash in them even in summertime. The time has come to reconsider the notion that a mosque is only a religious institution and to acknowledge that the mosque, both *de jure* and *de facto,* is primarily a social institution that influences all aspects of life and in many ways regulates all of daily life in the mahalla and the family. The mosque's decisive influence on the education of the young has already been examined, but its influence is no less real in other aspects of life.

The mazars are another group of religious institutions. The term *mazar* has a number of regional peculiarities. In Tajikistan, for example, the word is most often used to denote any holy place, while in western Turkmenistan the word means a place where people are buried, or a cemetery. Often the mazars have their own watchmen, who are the sheiks. Mazars are greatly respected all over Central Asia, and tradition accords many of them sacred powers. In Central Asia, Islam inherited a cult of mazars that had existed there long before the spread of Islam. The term *mazar* thus covers an enormous variety of structures, burial grounds, physical objects, trees, rocks, caves, springs, bodies of water, and simply places that people visit, but graveyards and graves have a particular significance. For a Muslim, burial grounds are always holy, provided of course that Muslims are buried there. The only distinction that is made is in the degree of sanctity, in the "power" of the buried "saint."

A mazar, or holy place, exists in practically every kishlak. Most commonly this is the graveyard, which of course every settlement possesses. Every graveyard inevitably has one grave that enjoys particular respect, in which the local "saint" is buried. There is no shortage of holy graves, which are formed in various ways. The grave may be that of the graveyard's founder (the first

100 THE ROLE OF RELIGION

grave in a new place), around whom a necropolis grows. In Turkmenistan such a grave must contain someone from one of the six "holy" tribes, or avlods, the holiness of which derives from their purported Arab origins, claims that undoubtedly have some basis. It is frequently said that these tribes trace their origins to one of the first six caliphs.*

All graves of the clergy, whether official or unofficial, are held to be sacred. Also holy are the graves of administrators of the emirates and khanates and those of the leaders of the Basmachi. For example, the grave of one of the leaders of the Basmachi movement, Enver Pasha, the minister of war for Turkey, has been declared holy, and no non-Muslim may approach it.†

That such "sacred" places form at the graves of people who fought actively against Soviet rule is a good indicator of the anti-Soviet nature of Central Asian Islamic culture. In thirty years of studying religious and burial sites, we have not found a single instance of the sanctification and revering of a grave of someone who fought to establish Soviet rule, let alone of the burial sites of communists. The best that may be hoped for is that their graves are not simply abandoned, and that occurs only if they are buried in settled areas.

New mazars are constantly being formed, but the sanctity of a mazar, unlike a mosque, is not transitory. Mazars are distinguished not only by their beneficial properties, their "powers," but also by their specificity. Some mazars "help avert" infertility,

---

*All Muslims accept the authority of the first four, or "rightly guided" caliphs (in Arabic *Khalifa,* the word for friend or representative). They were Abu Bakr, Umar, 'Uthman, and Ali, Muhammad's cousins and son-in-law. Supporters of Ali's sons Hassan and Hussein were hostile to Mu'awiya, who was the fifth caliph. When Yazid became the sixth caliph, a war broke out between supporters of the two groups. Those who supported the martyred Hussein became the Shi'a sect.

†Enver Pasha, minister of war in the pro-German Young Turk government during World War I, came to Soviet Russia to aid the Bolsheviks in taking control of Turkestan. Upon reaching Central Asia he changed sides, hoping to achieve his earlier pan-Turkic dreams. He died leading Basmachi forces in eastern Bukhara in August 1922. His grave is in southern Tajikistan, forty kilometers from the village of Baljuana.

others "cure" jaundice, or ear diseases, or rheumatism, and so forth. But the primary distinction among mazars is their "power," which is determined by the antiquity of the mazar and the degree of its sanctity. The essential value of a mazar is determined by a multitude of local conditions and causes. The fame of some mazars extends far back historically, as is the case with Paraubibi in the Kyzylarvat Raion of Turkmenistan and Suleimen's Mountain in Osh Oblast of Kyrgyzstan, which date from Arab times, and many others. Every region has its own "strong" mazar, to which residents of the surrounding area make pilgrimages.

The "power" and fame of a mazar are not defined by what is built around it. Stones, springs, graves, and other things can be "powerful," and of late there is emerging a curious hierarchy of holy places, some of which are equal to Mecca. Three visits to some of these, such as Suleimen's Mountain, is considered to be the equivalent of making *haj*, just as an ascent of the Boboi Mountains is considered to be three times "stronger" than a pilgrimage to other local mazars.

The great majority of mazars are in very good repair. Sometimes state money is used to restore them, as happened in the village of Chadak in Namangan Oblast in Uzbekistan, but usually the repair and upkeep of a "holy" place is borne by the local inhabitants. Any disrespect for a mazar provokes hostility, and local residents react especially sharply to disrespect shown by non-Muslims. At the same time, though, the neglected condition of local, secondary mazars causes local residents no particular concern. In most instances upkeep depends upon whether or not the mazar has a sheik.

One of the functions of the mazars is intercession between man and God. Two figures intercede at the same time, the "saint" to whom the mazar is dedicated and the sheik who is its guardian, or more precisely, master. The majority of mazars are in graveyards, regardless of the graveyard's size. A cemetery mazar does not have to have graves, though mazars with graves predominate. The sheik does not have to be in his "place of work."

Fifteenth-Century Grave (Mangyshlak)

The pilgrims know where to find him. Often the mazar is deliberately made to look neglected so that the local officials (financial inspectors are especially feared) will take the mazar to be non-functioning.

This increased incidence of graveyard mazars can be explained by longstanding Soviet laws that make religious rituals in a cemetery as legal as those conducted in a registered mosque, regardless of whether the leader of the ritual is officially registered as clergy or not.* In this regard it should be noted that an ever-increasing number of mazars, especially those that have buildings, are taking on the functions of mosques, because collective prayers are said there, even if on an irregular basis.

Mosques and mazars have their own budgets, financed by pay-

---

*In 1990 the USSR Supreme Soviet and many republic soviets began debating laws on "freedom of conscience," which removed most restrictions on religious practice. The USSR law subsequently passed, as did a number of similar republic bills.

Modern Grave (foreground) of Party Functionary, Surrounded by Traditional Tombs (Mangyshlak).

ments from parishioners and pilgrims and by the income from *waqf* lands (which belong to religious bodies). It has already been noted that waqf land is not subject to tax; the status of such lands is left undefined, so they simply exist on the collective farms, unregistered, and income from such lands goes to support the religious buildings and their clergy. Payments by parishioners are made in money and livestock that can be sold at the bazaars. Having their own money and livestock makes the religious institutions independent and allows the clergy to work at their "beneficent" jobs. If someone among the parishioners (in the mahalla) suddenly needs livestock for slaughtering, for example when an unexpected guest arrives, the sheik always has it. Although usurious interest (*riba*) is forbidden in Islam, repayment is always larger than the original amount.

One last point. Religious buildings generally have some sort of "screen" that hides what they are. In Varukh, for example, there are bakeries that make flat breads, right next to the functioning mosques and mazars, and the bakers watch over the holy sites. The major feature uniting mosques and mazars is that they continue to shape public opinion at the level of the village and of the mahalla. It is precisely at this level that the mosque and mazar have always worked and work today. It is for this reason that they must be studied at the level of the kishlak and of the mahalla.

14

The Clergy

> *Whoever joins other gods with God, God will forbid him the Garden, and the Fire will be his abode.*   The Koran, V, 75

There are two categories of mullah: official ones, who have completed the Bukhara medresseh, have been ordained, and have been registered by the proper representatives of the Muslim Spiritual Administration of Central Asia and Kazakhstan (SADUM); and unofficial ones, who have completed no school, save perhaps for a few years in an ordinary Soviet school, and at best have studied in an underground maktab. These latter are not registered as religious figures by the Soviet organs.

The social status of the two groups is different. The first group, who have diplomas, conduct their religious activities openly, on a legal basis, since they are registered to some sort of religious group. This group also experiences certain constraints, since they are required to observe Soviet laws on religion.*

The unregistered mullahs conduct their business with somewhat less pomp. They are recruited from among the students of the underground maktabs and often from among pensioners, but the majority of the underground imams in the unregistered mosques also have some "legal" job in the state or cooperative

---

*The material in this chapter reflects the state of affairs in 1989. As noted in the introduction to this book and in a note to the previous chapter, in 1990 many of the laws governing church–state relations changed. As a result many "unofficial clerics" became employed by SADUM.

sector. There are even schoolteachers among them, and it is no rarity that people occupying administrative posts in government offices become mullahs. In the past five years the activities of such mullahs have become increasingly legalized and the unregistered mosques are removing their wraps of "illegality."

As for the respective influence each group of mullahs, and the mosques they represent, has on the populace, it must be assumed that the two groups observe a precise division of labor. The pomp of the collective Friday prayers permits the official clergy to create a show of the greatness and unchanging significance of Islam. The sermons, rituals, and the mosque itself serve to demonstrate the "state-approved" nature of religion, where Islam simply represents the realization of the constitutional right of freedom of conscience that citizens of the USSR enjoy. Equally, as a religious body with its own structure and hierarchy, created in the Soviet period, the officially recognized part of Islam is the only aspect of the religion that comes under government control, with professional administration, as for example by SADUM.*

The division between "state-approved" and "unofficial" Islam is not absolute. Collective services in unregistered mosques are a common occurrence. For example, the imam of the state-sanctioned Leninabad mosque led such services in his native kishlak of Varukh in July 1985. The mullahs influence all aspects of the life of society through intermediaries, who constitute a sort of activitists' group. Thus the official clergy retain an extremely strong influence even on the people whose job it is to direct atheistic propaganda in their republics.

The activities of the unofficial clergy are neither controlled nor administered. Whereas the imam of a registered mosque meets with his parishioners only once a week, on Fridays (not counting holidays), the imams of the unregistered neighborhood and village mosques meet their parishioners every day, and sometimes more. Although their authority among the people is in no way

---

*This duality of power continues to be preserved even though many "unofficial clerics" have been recognized. The "official clerics" were compromised by their association with the party.

comparable to that of the official clergy, the imams of the unregistered, neighborhood mosques are the main foundation of Central Asian Islam. Even though the majority of such mullahs do not know dogma, the canonically approved rituals, or the prayers, they serve Islam very well on the daily level, because they know very well what *their* people need. They preserve *their* Islam, which consists of everything that satisfies *their* society. This Islam stands very successful guard over the customs described above and those that will be described below. Without "everyday Islam" and the unregistered mullahs, the showy Friday gatherings at the big city mosques would be half empty, the floors of the mosques covered, if at all, with reed mats, and certainly not the expensive carpets that cover them now.

A very important circumstance must be taken into account to understand the activities of the unofficial clergy: with very few exceptions all of the mullahs and sheiks come from traditional clerical families. It is on this same principle that students are chosen for the underground religious schools.

As in everything else having to do with Islam in Central Asia, a great deal here is determined by regional specifics. In some places, such as northern Tajikistan, the sheiks of the mazars are the children of mullahs, while in Turkmenistan they are descendants of the six "holy" tribes, and in Uzbekistan, Kazakhstan, and many regions of Tajikistan they are from the social ranks of the *haji* (those who have made pilgrimage) and *seids* (the honorific for descendants of Muhammad, who trace their origins through the Prophet's grandson Hussein). They consider themselves continuers of Muhammad. The descendants of Genghis Khan, the *tura*, also accept the post of sheik.

The vitality of these groups should be noted, particularly because of the privileges that Muslims acknowledge are due them. Descendants of the heads of the dervish orders also enjoy great respect, particularly those of the Nakhshabandiya order (a Sufi brotherhood named for its leader, Bakh ad-din Nakhshaban). Until the beginning of Soviet rule this order's leaders were among the richest people in Central Asia, if not the richest. These descendants are primarily concentrated in Samarkand, grouping particularly around the holy places, especially the mausoleum of Haji Ahrour, which is next to the clan's graveyard and mosque.

Traditionally the clergy divide up Central Asia, so that for example Mangyshlak is in Khorezm's purview, and religious personnel are recruited from there even today. Another example is the village of Varukh, which supplies clergy for many regions of western Fergana. Because of this division some regional specificity in observation of the religion is preserved, and has become traditional.

Sheiks have a very large influence on the population of Central Asia, because they are in constant contact with the people. This group of clergy is often overlooked in propaganda work, in scholarly studies, and in issuing directives. As has been noted, the sheiks' primary influence is on the female portion of society, since the majority of pilgrims to the mazars are women, who believe the keepers of the mazars without question. It is here that the main shaper of children gets the values that she then transfers to the younger generation.

Unlike the conduct of rituals in the mosques, which can be simple but is never unregulated, everything at the mazars is easy and free, just as at home. The way in which emotions are expressed depends entirely upon the pilgrims, and the services that are demanded are quite familiar and domestic—slaughter an animal, prepare food, request something of the "saint," and pay the sheik the sum thought necessary for his intercession. The pilgrim always finds a warm reception at the mazar.

As was noted, recently in many regions of Central Asia there has been a clear tendency for mosques and mazars to merge, which also merges the functions of sheik and mullah. In the past, meaning fifteen to twenty years ago, this would have been considered impossible; the sheik who had a mazar almost never visited the mosque, but prayed instead at the mazar. The "sanctity" of the mazar was (and remains) incomparably stronger than the "sanctity" of the mosque, which, incidentally, is yet another demonstration of the mosque's "state-property" quality.

The expedition's field materials show that this merger of mosque and mazar, like that of mullah and sheik, is brought about by legalization of the mazar's functions. Under this mantle the mazar has in turn legalized the activity of the unregistered mosques. Since the great majority of mosques are located next to cemeteries, each of which has a mazar, religious groups have no need to register. Officially services take place at the mazar in the cemetery, which the law permits; in fact they are taking place in the mosque. In addition, many mazars have outside awnings that have *mikhrabs*, (indicating the direction of Mecca), and in summertime group prayers are conducted there, further hidden by the high thick walls that separate cemeteries from the outside world in towns and villages. The local village organs of both government and party know all about such practices and do nothing to prevent them, in the best of circumstances pretending only that nothing is happening. It may be said with certainty that by now entire *dynasties* of clergy have been founded in Central Asia, primarily in the unofficial sector. Imams for the unregistered mosques are named in a reasonably democratic manner: they are elected, primarily by the elders. It is not uncommon that an imam is removed from his post because his personal qualities do not meet the norms of village morals. This occurred, for example, in the village of Metk, in the Ganchin Raion of Tajikistan. The sheik's greed finally led parishioners to hold an open meeting at which they fired him and elected a new man for the job.

There is a real battle for the job of sheik at a well-known mazar, which provides a large income. This can take an odd twist, such as when candidates ask Soviet authorities to intercede as arbiters. This seemingly comic situation says a great deal about the legalization of the mazars as socially necessary institutions, which means the sheiks do not fear to turn to the Soviet authorities, who in their turn perceive the mazars to be fulfilling a normal function and so do not close these religious institutions, which are functioning in violation of Soviet law.

An important and very influential figure in Central Asian Islam is the bibiotun (or otyncha), with one in every mahalla of every settlement. The job of the bibiotun is to oversee all the female rituals in the mahalla. It is usually taken by a woman who has been specially prepared for the role. In addition to absolutely thorough knowledge of the rituals, she must know the norms of good (Muslim) behavior and be able to read the Arabic alphabet. Our materials suggest that many of the bibiotun do not know Arabic, but practically all of them know Arabic script. It also seems that the younger the bibiotun, the higher her educational qualifications.

Candidates for the post of bibiotun are chosen from among girls seven to eight years old, who then go through the same preparation in the girls' maktabs as the boys who will become the future mullahs do in theirs. Every bibiotun has from one to three pupils, girls from her neighborhood, who must be from "good" families. Given the existing system of marriage arrangement, at least one of these girls will remain in her own neighborhood after her training and so inherit the post of bibiotun. Just as the boy who will be the future unregistered mullah knows his flock from childhood, so too does the bibiotun know hers. If a girl who has been trained should move into another neighborhood after marriage, she can also perform the function of bibiotun there. These women are in general highly respected among Muslims. So far we have not been able to define the mechanism of how "zones of influence" are distributed when there are two bibiotuns in one mahalla, but it seems that only one of them serves, or at least plays the major role.

The various "descendants" of the Prophet, the caliphs and so forth, who have already been mentioned, also make up an enormously large group of unofficial clergy and enjoy great influence. Because of their ancestry and without regard for how much they know about Islam (or how little, as is often the case), these men can conduct all the religious services. They are among the most fanatical adherents of Islam, prepared to do anything to retain their privileges. It must be remembered that the privileges of this self-selected clergy are not fictitious but real, although how those privileges are expressed in different regions and situations demands a special investigation. These descendants are the most active "propaganda brigade" of Islam and agitate constantly among the population.

The system through which observation of all the canonical and, even more so, noncanonical norms of Islam is supervised (or overseen, more exactly) is precisely elaborated, taken over now by the neighborhood committees. Our materials suggest that in the regions of the Fergana valley we studied the neighborhood committees were in fact beyond the control and influence of the state. That control exists only on paper, while the neighborhood committees know precisely the moods of the people and the political inclinations of the government offices. For example, the neighborhood committees fought drunkenness fairly seriously by introducing alcohol-free celebration of the holidays (tois). A gathering of elders would decide to limit the number of alcoholic beverages that could be purchased for guests, and in a few places they even limited the sale of alcohol. Nevertheless, these sorts of decisions are often overlooked, so that good intentions, unsupported by consistent work, have no effect. At the same time the neighborhood committees do nothing to interfere with the illegal showing of pornographic films or the dissemination of audio tapes with recordings of "religious" songs.

In some places, such as Uzbekistan, the neighborhood committees are elected by the residents of the mahalla, which means in practice that the most respected elders become members of the committee. In a number of places, in order to satisfy the letter of the law, the neighborhood committees include *one* woman. This is done purely for show, and such women take no part in the committees' work. In some places, though not many, it is the bibiotun (or otyncha) who is elected to the committee. At present, membership in the neighborhood committees can sometimes bring a certain income, which can be fairly large for the president. Primarily this income is "payment" for advice, for agreeing to "take measures," and so forth. An over-all description of the activities of the neighborhood committees would have to conclude that to a great (albeit variable) degree they help strengthen

Islamic customs and maintain the old traditional way of life. Even lip service to "progressive principles" is quite infrequent, and the neighborhood committees undertake their activities in closer cooperation with the clergy than with the government and Party organs. In their daily activities the neighborhood committees work hand in hand with the older generation of the mahalla, the mothers-in-law and the senior men. These are the people who actively form public opinion in the mahalla, on all subjects.

Nor should it be overlooked that the clergy actively interfere in personnel policy and the formation of public opinion. Numerous examples exist. Their period of "regrouping of forces" has ended, and the Muslim clergy have begun to attack Soviet practices and to legalize their own activities. The economic basis of Islam definitely exists, in the form of petty commodity production, and there is no shortage of cadres for propagandizing Islam. Recruitment among women and youth has become particularly active. During the expedition we were able to collect field material about active pro-Islamic agitation by girls who had completed studies with a bibiotun (or otyncha). The nature of this agitation shows clearly that it is designed for women, and that its primary goal is to convince them of the necessity of preserving the old "national" ways. This again shows Islam's very great attention to the education of children, but it should also be remembered that these women are the future grandmothers and mothers-in-law who, as practice shows, will continue to set the tone of education for the younger generation and set the practices of the family and of the mahalla.

V

SOCIAL DYNAMICS OF TRADITIONALISM

15

Traditionalism and the Working Class

> *Our Lord! lay not on us a burden greater than we have strength to bear.*
>   The Koran, II, 286

Traditionalism sees the working class as its main enemy. All the processes that slow the development of a national working class are refined and celebrated by tradition. Early marriages are an example of this policy. Particularly common in the villages, early marriage closes off a young man's opportunity to learn an industrial skill. He cannot get the education he needs in the village, but he cannot leave the village, because he has to feed his family. Poor command of Russian also plays a large role here, making it more difficult for a young man to acquire an industrial specialty that can be used outside of his own republic. Early marriages deprive youth of social mobility and tie them to the village. As has been noted, young families cannot exist without the assistance of the parents, because they still do not have their "own" land, which means that the land does not provide the necessary quantity of cash goods, and hence there is no income on which to live. Because of overpopulation there are no jobs in the villages other than cultivating cash crops and selling them at market. As a result, a young man has to begin by working on his father's land in order to eat.

    Instructive in this regard is the contention of one of the first collective farm presidents in the village Metk (in the Ganchin Raion of the Tajikistan), who says that the mechanization of agriculture is a large part of the reason why there is so much unemployment in the villages. In the past, before the war, when plowing was done with oxen, there was work enough for everyone, but now plowing is done with tractors and people have nothing to do. This extremely important observation has great significance for all of Central Asia, because throughout Central Asia industrialization was introduced from the outside, very rapidly and categorically. The people proved unprepared to accept the change, since most of society was still at a level where new means of production were unnecessary. This barrier between the traditional agricultural family economy (in which 70 percent of the population is engaged) and the modern urban industrial economy has not only not diminished, but has grown, as practice shows. In addition, income from the private plots is significantly larger than wages in industry. People often say that "It is better to earn fifty rubles in a state farm than two hundred in the city." They consider leaving the village and moving into the city only in extreme circumstances. In "profitable" settlements, where apricots are grown, for example, the shortage of land suitable for growing this crop is so great that houses have begun to push up, into the air. Most of the dwellings are already two-storied, and there are now some attempts to add a third story, at least for summer use. Traditionalism takes a very active part in urging young people to settle in close proximity to their parents, with significant success.

An industrial profession tears a worker from the economic and social environment of the village, where traditionalism is the dominant ideology. An industrial worker's economic independence from the mahalla also defines his freedom from the village social environment. Participating in industrial production demands, assists, and makes possible the improvement of one's professional level. It creates internationalist consciousness, eliminates traditionalism's exclusivity, and simply makes it possible for a person to get a variety of reliable information about the real world. The mobility of an industrial worker is incomparably higher than that of a kishlak dweller. The latter is bound to his plot of land (and to petty commodity production), while the former is freed from agrarian property, which essentially is private. The villager has an interest in seeing that public production of potatoes, for example, is as low as possible, in order to raise prices at the market, while the worker is extremely interested in increasing public production, as Marxist theory demonstrates exhaustively. It is crucial that account be taken of this fact when considering the situation in Central Asia today.*

Work in an industrial plant and life in a workers' settlement or town severs those family ties that are based on petty commodity production and deprive the system of both its economic and its social basis. This is true not only for the male part of the population, but for the female part too, if the women are working in industrial enterprises. The Isfara Raion of Leninabad Oblast in Tajikistan is an instructive example, since almost all the possible varieties of adaptation to industrial production may be found among the villagers there.

Traditionalism is most fully weakened in industrial settlements like the new town of Communist Youth International (KIM), which is located next to an electrical engineering industrial complex. This expanding industry has had an enormous positive effect on the population of the neighboring villages, as has already been mentioned. I was able to lecture in the town, and to speak with many female workers, whom I found to be mothers and grandmothers quite unlike those who are still sitting behind their duvals back in the villages (the *duval* is the blind clay or brick wall of a traditional Muslim house; it must be taller than a man and shields the interior yard from the street and from the neighbors). The situation in the kishlak of Kuchkak, in the same region, is also much better than it is in nearby settlements. According to our observations, the main guardians of tradition in Kuchkak are the men.

Traditionalism is also significantly weakened in the mining set-

---

*Poliakov has gone so far as to argue that the government in Central Asia (and elsewhere) turns a blind eye to the destruction of "public" crops (collective farm produce for sale in state stores) to ensure that private plot prices are kept high, thus preserving the network for bribery of officials.

tlement of Shurabe. Our limited field material about this settlement does not permit us to draw final conclusions about the situation in Shurabe today, but it is already clear that traditionalism there is in retreat (making allowances for the conditions of Central Asia).

Big changes have also occurred in the village of Nefteabad (Oil City) in the same region. In oil-worker families the fathers insist that their daughters continue their educations, not only in Leninabad and Dushanbe but even in Moscow and in other cities of the USSR. It is true that the mothers are frequently against it, but often to no avail. It has to be noted, however, that Nefteabad also has many seid families, whose members join the ranks of the Muslim clergy. Nevertheless it is clear that in this case "everyday Islam" is not able to compete with industrialization.

In Isfara itself there are marked differences in the behavior of families whose members work in industry and those in other enterprises. The more collective the process of labor, the less traditionalism there is. It is possible to distinguish at least three kinds of departures from traditionalism, as illustrated by three different industrial enterprises: a motor-transport depot, a sewing factory, and a metallurgical industrial complex. The degree of traditionalism's influence varies from place to place, being the greatest at the depot and the least at the metallurgical plant. A worker's place of residence influences the significance that the old ways have in his daily life. Those who live in new settlements preserve the "national customs" to a significantly lesser degree than those who do not. There are many examples of this. For instance, in Ashkhabad, the railroad serves as a kind of demarcation line dividing the city into two halves, the northern, where private houses predominate, and the southern, which is a modern city with high-rise buildings. According to information received from the personnel of a raion committee of the Communist party of Turkmenistan, tradition is incomparably stronger among the people of the northern half than it is among those in the southern half of the city. This means that industrial housing has great importance, which explains why traditionalism so greatly fears industrialization of daily life.

This touches upon an important unresolved theoretical problem, the interrelationship of city and village in Central Asia, the degree to which the city is separated from the village, and the mutual influence between urban and rural populations. Our materials show that to deal effectively with social processes, including demographic ones, it is necessary to divide the concept of the city into several levels. The relations that may be found between rural inhabitants of the Akhal oasis and residents of Ashkhabad in Turkmenistan are very different from those which exist between the city of Ura-tiube and its environs in Tajikistan. It is only possible to understand general processes when one knows the specifics of the immediate locale, the oblast, the raion and so on.

The corruptive influence of the petty commodity economy also affects the working class. In Samarkand, for example, a system has developed in which young men are hired to work through the winter in the industrial plants of the city, leaving in spring for the start of spring agricultural work on the private plots. The majority of these people received their industrial training while serving in the Soviet Army, but are not to be seen in the factories until November. This is not a new problem. It has been thoroughly discussed in the press, and state, party and Komsomol organs have all promised to correct the situation and have even issued the necessary resolutions. But so far matters continue unchanged. These seasonal workers also take every possible advantage of the factory, getting rich by taking private orders "on the side" to make the goods necessary for the petty commodity economy. Thus the jobs that are most highly prized are not those at the large factories, where discipline is stricter and labor better organized, but at the smaller, less significant places, where work "on the side" is considered the norm. It must again be presumed that official statistics count such seasonal workers as factory hands, distorting the figures on which social policy is based.

For Central Asia as a whole, the national working class has essentially no influence on the development of society, or a very small one at best. Undoubtedly one cause for this is the very small number of workers who come from the indigenous population. Another is the extremely close connection that such native workers as there are maintain with the village. A great many workers, even in large industrial centers like Leninabad (in Tajikistan), live in a mahalla, meaning in those parts of the city that have preserved the old ways and customs, where the influence of traditionalism is very strong.

Another important reason why the national working class has so little influence on the life of society as a whole is that the majority of the indigenous workers are first-generation or, very rarely, second-generation workers.

Unfortunately, it must also be said that negative interethnic tendencies are beginning to appear among the working class. Amicable personal contacts between Muslims and non-Muslims outside of work hours are becoming ever rarer. Where such contacts were fairly firm and relatively frequent among the older generation, who are already pensioners now, they are significantly weaker and less frequent among the younger generation. Here again the "mahalla factor" must be noted, as it is precisely among those workers who live in a mahalla (in a city) that interethnic contacts outside of work time are the most attenuated.

Industrial production in Central Asia is based on "imported" workers and residents who are not from the indigenous population; the skilled work force both for those industrial enterprises that are being built and for those that are already functioning is primarily recruited outside of Central Asia. Large numbers of skilled workers come from outside to work on large-scale construction projects and in facilities such as the Regarskii Metallurgical Industrial Complex.

Central Asia has a very great shortage of qualified workers in civil construction, which has recently grown worse; this deterioration exposes another problem, that of the graduates of technical training schools (PTUs). For example, in the Andijan Oblast of Uzbekistan, a great many of the PTU graduates who have degrees in industrial specialties do not work in factories. Here we encounter the same reasons given above: that to do so would mean moving to the city and leaving the parents behind, for a starting salary that is not very large. As we have seen, a young man may earn very handsomely on a private plot. Not only has poor planning in this regard meant wasted money, it has also had bad consequences for the social situation. Work of any sort in Central Asia must be right next to where one lives. The choice between moving to a far-off city where there is work and remaining in the village where there is not always work favors staying put. If they go to the city, young men (there is no possibility whatever of girls doing so, of course) have to change their entire way of life, for which sixteen- and seventeen-year-olds are ill prepared. Parents and children alike are particularly frightened of dormitory life.

Another problem, housing, is just as critical in questions of attracting a work force from outside. It is not by chance that the resolution on development of housing construction in Central Asia issued by the CPSU Central Committee and the USSR Council of Ministers stresses cities, such as Dushanbe. In many places the housing problem has acquired a political character, since population growth among the indigenous population greatly outstrips even the total amount of housing being built, but only a fraction of the new housing is allotted to the indigenous population. A large part of new housing goes to the newcomers, workers recruited from outside. This practice does nothing to win over the indigenous population or to strengthen friendship among peoples. As has been noted, housing construction is hampered by the lack of highly qualified workers in the construction industry. There are simply not enough workers. This problem became especially acute after the earthquake in northern Tajikistan, where, despite massive governmental assistance from the outside in the form of construction materials, the reconstruction is proceeding at a snail's pace, which permits traditionalism to influence the social and economic situation of the region.*

This ever growing shortage of workers in republics that have

---

*The acute housing shortage is one explanation that has been given for the political activism of youth in both Frunze (Bishkek) and Dushanbe.

absolute and relative overpopulation and an enormous surplus of unqualified workers is becoming increasingly severe. Solving this problem would seem to be of paramount importance if the situation in Central Asia is ever to be normalized; unfortunately, of late the situation has become even more complex, as skilled workers who are not from ethnic groups indigenous to Central Asia try to move out of the region.*

---

*The outmigration of Europeans has greatly accelerated since Poliakov completed his manuscript.

16

Traditionalism and the Intelligentsia

Truly fancy can be of no avail against Truth. The Koran, X, 37

To understand the situation among the national intelligentsia in Central Asia it is necessary to understand how people are trained for the various professions. The situation with elementary education in Central Asia has been fairly well described in the central press. Until recently, schoolchildren throughout Central Asia spent two months a year harvesting cotton. Although this practice is now being discontinued, in the past children lost twelve months or more of school time over the course of their elementary education, or the equivalent of a grade and a half. Thus, in most rural schools the children got just eight-plus grades instead of the ten-grade education the state requires.

Despite numerous promises from the leaders of the Central Asian republics that students will not be used in the cotton-harvesting campaign, this practice continues even today. So far discussion of restructuring education has gone no further than good intentions.*

In many regions parents simply do not send their children to school after the fifth or sixth grade, considering that they have sufficient education once they can read, write, and do sums. This

---

*Poliakov may be minimizing the improvement in the child labor situation that has occurred in recent years. Nonetheless, the use of child labor in Central Asia, especially at harvest time, remains widespread.

is the case, for example, in the kishlak of Metk, in Ganchin Raion, Leninabad Oblast, Tajikistan. The reasoning is always the same: "I didn't have an education [the speaker being no more than forty years old], yet I live better [or 'have more money'] than the teacher. My children should work at home." It is true that the petty commodity economy is in constant need of workers (its exploitation of child labor has been mentioned above). A man's entire social position is also determined by the rubles in his coffers. The respect he commands is directly proportional to the thickness of his wallet. Nor is it uncommon that the people who become teachers are barely able to read a newspaper themselves.

It is not my goal here to attempt any sort of detailed survey of the state of elementary education in Central Asia. I simply offer these examples to indicate the real level of preparation for most graduates of the Central Asian schools. The inadequacy of this level for modern requirements is eloquently demonstrated, for example, by the students who come to Moscow from the Central Asian republics, to occupy guaranteed places in the History Faculty of Moscow State University. There are undoubtedly a few well-prepared students among them, but most are inadequate in the extreme.

The training of advanced students is no better in the Central Asian republics. A few institutes and universities produce graduates who can stand up to comparison with specialists trained in most of the institutions of higher education in the country, but in general the disorganization of the rural economy in Central Asia has been very detrimental. The length of most students' studies is considerably shortened, and their mastery of their subjects is far from satisfactory. One example is the graduates of the pedagogical institutes, who when they begin to work in the schools then produce low-quality students. I am not so bold as to criticize the skills of specialists in all fields and at all levels, and so speak only of the social sciences and humanities, which is the situation with which I am most familiar.

There are also problems in the preparation of specialists at the highest levels. At best, graduates of local institutes of higher learning are sent for graduate work to institutions in Moscow, Leningrad, and other leading scientific centers of the country, where the academic institutes are especially active in enrolling such students. In spite of the fact that these students do a minimum of two additional years of preparatory work before moving on to graduate work proper, the quality of such scholars still leaves a great deal to be desired. What elementary and secondary education has not supplied cannot be remedied in graduate study. In general what occurs is that scholarly culture is simply crippled. In quantitative terms there would seem to be enough specialists with advanced degrees, but qualitatively they do not satisfy modern requirements.

At present in Central Asia the number of specialists in the natural sciences is not proportionate to the numbers in the social sciences and humanities; the great majority of the indigenous intelligentsia receive their degrees in the latter fields. There is very stiff competition for places in the humanities and social-sciences faculties of the Central Asian institutions of higher education, but a chronic shortage of indigenous students for the natural science and technical specialties.

A humanities degree is no particular threat to tradition. Over time, in fact, for the academic institutions of Central Asia the humanities and social sciences have become "national" specialties. In the historical disciplines, for example, most of the scholars study the history of their own people or that of the peoples in neighboring countries. Ancient and medieval history, archaeology, and ethnography are by far the most popular courses of study, and very little work is undertaken on questions that go beyond the bounds of the particular republic's history. This means in turn that publications are only about the history of one's own people, under the dominating conviction that all that is "ours" is good, combined with a definite tendency to inflate everything that is good so that it is portrayed as perfect. Here we see in full force how the basic disposition, referred to above, to reject everything that is not traditional, is expressed in education, where it may be found in various guises in a number of works.

Unfortunately, this creates an atmosphere of greatly exaggerated claims for their cultural richness by each of the various peoples, with consequent marking off of "national boundaries" (that is, nationalism). The stimuli for this phenomenon have not been aired or seriously analyzed, nor has it been noted how nationalism has become a reality even in scholarly studies in the humanities and social sciences. The concept of a "golden age" is widespread, by which is meant the period before Central Asia was joined to Russia, and scholars speak with some reservations about a "silver age," during the time of the Russian empire, but never do any of them speak positively of the Soviet period. If absolutely forced to discuss it, they will pay lip service to the thesis, which is far from conclusively proven, that tsarist Russia threatened the peoples of the Central Asian periphery with extinction.

Like it or not, the humanities and social sciences are now working to further traditionalism, since scholars are avoiding (or perhaps are being steered away from?) the most pressing and most important ideological problems. This is the real state of things, and to ignore this does nothing but further the mundane essence of tradition. To see that this is true requires only an examination of what scholarly publications and dissertations are written about, and in what way. Traditionalism protects itself from any criticism with a strong wall of taboos.

It should be remembered too that the history of the Central Asian peoples is studied primarily in Central Asia. Only Central Asian archaeology has been subjected to serious scientific scrutiny, and that only at a certain level, for a whole range of regional reasons that demand special study. The other subdivisions of history, such as ethnography, are almost entirely monopolized by Central Asian scientific centers.

Civil historians of Central Asia and scholars studying political history feel even more unfettered, because no one else is working on their topics. The state of historical science in Central Asia now is such that only an insignificantly small number of scholars do quantitative work; most use traditional descriptive methods. This creates broad avenues for subjective evaluation and interpretation of past events, even of entire epochs and of the historical paths of peoples. It has also led to extremely dangerous competition in claiming cultural heritages, in setting priorities for political history, and in evaluating the social and economic development attained by the large, numerous peoples and by those small in number. This competition further exacerbates nationalistic moods.

The absence of alternative studies and its consequences are plainly visible in the analysis of Russia's role in the history of Central Asia, mentioned above. While the passing of Central Asia to Russian control is described in standard phrases about how this union was essentially progressive, it is also argued that the policies of Russian tsarism were leading the populations of the "peripheral colonies" toward extinction; among these, it is invariably claimed, were the peoples of Central Asia, who were saved only by the coming of Soviet power. This has become a standard explanation, a textbook staple at all levels. None of the Central Asian scholars have made any attempt to examine the real consequences of Central Asia's being joined with Russia, especially the consequences for Central Asian agriculture. However, even a cursory look at the published census materials will show that in the first fifty years after Central Asia was joined to Russia the native population not only did not diminish, let alone come close to extinction, but rather increased more than threefold. This particular example may be said to characterize the entire trend of such scholarship. Similarly, all the textbooks and surveys of history devote a lot of space to the spread of Islam in Central Asia and to the Islamization of the population. This tendency became particularly strong after the 1960s. Without linking the two processes at the moment, I would note that this process of the "nationalization" of history was accompanied by the "legalization" of "everyday Islam"—meaning the activity of the unregistered clergy and their mosques.

To a great degree the development of negative phenomena in

the social sciences in Central Asia is promoted by the concepts behind the research and writing of textbooks on the history of the USSR as this is done in the leading academic and educational centers of Moscow, Leningrad, and other cities. These texts depict the history of the USSR as the history of the Russian government from the time of Kievan Rus or, less commonly, from the time of the first appearance of the Slavs in the Dnieper basin. By this same time, however, governments, developed literacy, science, and professional art had all been long established in Central Asia and the Caucasus. An example of this approach is a 600-page text on the history of the USSR, edited by Professor V.V. Mavrodin,[19] in which Central Asia is given fewer than 30 pages. What kind of internationalism is this?

Of course, we should not conclude that all scholars of the social sciences and humanities in the Central Asian republics are nationalists, but reality is such that any reasonably begun historical study is generally lost among concepts for which the theoretical premises are doubtful. The fight over "cultural heritage" has taken such forms that well-reasoned scientific polemic is impossible. For example, at a scientific conference dedicated to the 2,500th anniversary of Khodzhent,* one of the corresponding members of the Tajik Academy of Sciences announced from the podium, in everyone's hearing, that from the eleventh through the nineteenth century the language spoken by most of the population of India was Tajik-Persian! None of those present at the session spoke out against this wild absurdity because the speaker had been introduced by the head of the republic Academy of Sciences as a patriot and important scientist. This was not merely a curious incident: there were many students present at the session, teachers-to-be, who will take this nonsense all over the republic, where it will be absorbed by their pupils in the schools.

The exacerbation of nationalistic feelings works objectively in favor of traditionalism, which cannot accept cordial interethnic relations.

---

*Leninabad was renamed Hojant (Khodzhent) in 1991.

The technical intelligentsia, who by nature are more internationalist, are extremely few in number among the indigenous populations of Central Asia. On the everyday level, choice of a technical profession is often discouraged, for a number of reasons. Primary among them is how difficult such professions are for most graduates of the rural schools. Even those technical professions that may be learned in the PTUs can be mastered by only a few of the young men, because of the poor preparation they receive in the rural middle schools. Of course, conditions are not the same in all regions, but in general the situation in technical education is alarming. Traditionalism also plays a large, albeit hidden, role in discouraging technical education, because pursuing a technical education and training for an industrial career almost automatically tears an individual away from rural society and from the way of life that dominates there. This means too that the everyday bonds between the generations are disrupted as children leave the influence of their parents and the rural mahallas. The importance of these two social institutions in society's functioning in Central Asia has already been discussed.

There is another aspect to the question. Technical specialties demand a reasonably free command of Russian, without which it is impossible to obtain new (professional) information. In recent years the teaching of Russian in most rural schools has been extremely poor, so that most young people have been cut off from the heritage of world culture and are deprived of new information, which is the basis of modern development in society.

Furthermore, because of their material nature, technical specialities in particular (like those in the natural sciences in general) are much less susceptible to subjectivity than are the humanities; they are more objective. This in turn makes it very much more difficult to accept the existence of a "divine origin."

Finally, technical specialists who work in industry and in proletarian collectives are not as susceptible as village laborers to the influence of traditionalism and are not tied directly to petty commodity production.

Indirect and direct ties between the urban intelligentsia and the rural population are very persistent, just as on the whole the Central Asian city is closely tied to the village. These ties are historically established, and only rarely has city separated from village to become a qualitatively new entity. In most regions direct family ties continue to prevail between urban and rural residents, because the petty commodity economy of the village also feeds the urban intelligentsia. As practice has shown, the village has the greatest influence upon those in the humanities.

The influence of traditionalism on the intelligentsia is increased by the very poor training students get in the middle schools and institutions of higher education in Central Asia. Although some specialists are well trained, they are rare, and most cadres are simply "stamp-pressed" out by the schools and do not meet even the most minimal of standards. These graduates then go to work in the schools or the factories, where they produce defective goods. When a worker is unable to do his job properly, connections of family and birthplace become of paramount importance in holding on to it, particularly if it is highly paid. Such connections are regenerated and cultivated in the village, while ability to do the job, assuming no candidates have higher educational status, is the least important consideration of all.

The "men of respect" in the mahalla also influence personnel policy, with traditional piety being one of the most important factors. A proof of this is the very large percentage of those in the social sciences and humanities who are descendants of haji, sheiks, and ishans, groups that in the past enjoyed a monopoly in clerical titles and posts. To some degree this also includes the *tura*, the descendants of Genghis Khan. On the everyday level such hereditary status is greatly respected. It is not uncommon, and in some places it is the rule, for leading and aspiring scholars to be recruited from among these groups. It is of course indiscriminate to accuse all descendants of the haji and other "holy" groups of being proponents of traditionalism, but practice demonstrates that positions of authority are frequently used to do exactly that: promote tradition.

Traditionalism in "national culture" presents a particular danger, although the field is so broad that any sort of thorough examination of tradition's place in world culture would require a work of many volumes. Here I will only attempt to delineate what I think are the most important aspects of the link between traditionalism and the culture of a people.

For example, the opinion now current among scholars that Islam as a system created an "Islamic culture" must be regarded as a misunderstanding, based primarily on a literature from the end of the nineteenth century and, early twentieth century, when archaeology was making its first steps in serious interpretation of the data it was discovering, and could not yet fully elaborate the historical truth.

Based primarily Arabic and Persian historical sources (which are "Islamic"), the history understood then was a half-truth, although, like it or not, even today in Central Asia the idea of some sort of "ancient crisis" that supposedly was averted by the Arab conquest is widely current. On its face this thesis is absurd, and no one defends it in this "bald" form, but there is no difficulty in proving from textbooks on Central Asian history that Central Asia was "culturally insignificant" before the Arab conquest. Apart from Sogda and Khorezm, these texts say nothing of pre-conquest history.

Contrasting what the literature says about pre-Islamic history with the accumulated archaeological evidence should dispel any confusion and demonstrate how unfounded it is to speak of the constructive role of Islam. This, however, goes unremarked, for now, just as in the past, Islam exaggerates its constructive mission, as well as the benefits it brings to society. The basic tendency of the Islamic presentation of culture is to claim that all of mankind's cultural values were created by Islam. This claim is buttressed by various means and devices. The first, already discussed, is to cut the Muslim off from any knowledge that might cast doubt on claims about the constructive role of Islam, especially knowledge coming from "kafir" (meaning Soviet) sources. A second is to destroy by any means and methods anyone who bears "non-Islamic" information.

This tendency in Islam has deep roots. The priceless libraries of the pre-Arab period, the pagan priests, the scientists and poets of pre-Arab Central Asia were all reservoirs of human knowledge and experience, and it was precisely they whom the Arab conquerors destroyed. Today's texts devote much more space to the history of the spread of Islam than they do to explaining and analyzing the history of the *magi,* who were Islam's main opponents. In general the pre-Arab elements of medieval Central Asian culture are increasingly being emphasized in scholarship as "cultural connections." Such connections existed, of course, but Central Asia is often portrayed as an empty vessel into which the Arab "benefactors" from the southwest poured their healing balm.

The consequences of this approach have not been slow to appear, as one falsehood gives rise to another. Thus at the Second Convention of Turkologists in Alma-Ata in 1976, one academician (from the Kazakh Academy of Sciences) announced from the podium that the Mongol Genghis Khan was a Muslim, and that when at home in his tent he spoke Kazakh, an announcement that the majority of those present greeted with awe. In the context of such a meeting, the attitude was obvious that the Kazakhs should be proud of this notorious historical figure, because he was their countryman. Nor was this scientific gathering disturbed by the fact that in the thirteenth century there was still no evidence of the existence of an independent Kazakh language. What was paramount was that Genghis Khan was a Muslim. True, in this case the cultural influence flows from the east, so another example might be offered: that the Uzbeks should be proud of being related to Timur, the "sovereign of the faithful," who destroyed not only the lands he conquered, but Central Asia as well. This contention was the leitmotif of the showy celebration in honor of Timur conducted in Soviet Central Asia. At the same time the centenary of the poet of Khamza in Uzbekistan was much more modest, and with considerable reservations about the man being honored, reservations that persist.

It is vigorously argued that the Arab conquest was beneficial for all the peoples of the Arab caliphate, and the conquerors are presented as bearers of an advanced social structure and a leading culture, an exceptional phenomenon instead of just one wave of the worldwide circulation of nomadic herders, which had begun long before history reached the "Arab stage."

Even today the Arab language remains synonymous with education, and Muslims hold that only that knowledge permits a scholar to do fully valuable work in the humanities. It is becoming increasingly common to hear it argued at scholarly conferences that the study of Arabic literature should be obligatory in the middle schools of the Central Asian republics.

Supporters claim that this study is necessary to bridge a gap in the cultural sequence, but if that were the case, Sogdian and Pehlev literature should be studied first, because Sogdian was the language of the population of the Zeravshan valley until the ninth century and the ancestor of the language of the Yagnobs, descendants of the Sogdians who still live in small numbers in Tajikistan today. The Sogdian manuscripts that have survived are written in several alphabets—Manichean, Syrian, and Uguritic. Pehlev writing was based upon Aramaic figures, and was used for documents written in Middle Persian (from the fourth century B.C. to the eighth century A.D.).

However, while public opinion very actively supports the idea of studying Arabic, the study of Russian, which would open access to international contact and to knowledge of the modern achievements of world culture, is frowned on by the older generation in many regions of Central Asia, such as rural Andijan Oblast of Uzbekistan. In fact, parents consider enrolling children in schools where Russian is the language of instruction to be a prohibited or anti-Islamic act. Poor knowledge of Russian makes it practically impossible for children to get information that is not controlled by the mahalla (that is, by Islam). Children in the kishlaks and auls know Russian very poorly, which, as has been noted, is one cause of their lack of social mobility.

In these conditions traditionalism takes upon itself the mission of preserving "cultural traditions" beneath the armor of "national culture," which so far has been a reliable protection against critics, since the main thrust of studies of traditionalism is against its "state" form, which does not exist in the USSR. Neither the Institute of Oriental Studies of the Academy of Sciences of the USSR, the republic academies of sciences, the institutions of higher learning, nor any other institutions are seriously studying and criticizing domestic traditionalism. This was reflected in the conference organized by the Institute of Oriental Studies of the Academy of Sciences and the Institute of Scientific Atheism of the Academy of Social Sciences, on 14–15 October 1986, where of the twenty papers presented only one (by a representative of the Council of Religious Affairs of the USSR Council of Ministers) touched directly on the Soviet Union.

In such circumstances it is very easy to pass off pan-Islamism, pan-Turkism, and anti-Russian nationalism as part of "national culture," as the scholarly literature depicts it. Taken together, all these "isms" form an anti-Soviet background that is far from innocent. Such attitudes are actively encouraged by foreign pro-Islamic propaganda, which has become particularly vigorous since the events in Iran and Afghanistan.

Unfortunately, the administrative organs and the scientific institutions often underestimate the influence of foreign propaganda, or else overreact to it. This is the case with the broadcasts of the Iranian radio station Gorgan, which presents the unabashedly pan-Islamic concept of a Shi'ite (Islamic) government as being part of national cultural traditions.

Some people downplay the danger of Gorgan's broadcasts by arguing that the Turkmens, like the rest of the peoples of Central Asia, profess Sunni Islam, but this is convincing only for those who do not know the historical past. Shi'ism, at least on the everyday level, was widespread among the Turkmens as recently as the eighteenth century, and traces of it are still so strong in the Turkmen environment that there is even a saying, "When the Turkmen prays, the Uzbek spits," meaning that the Sunni Uzbeks do not accept the Shi'ite aspects of Turkmen Sunnism. There are many similar examples.

Moreover, the question is not just of quantity, but of the qualitative changes which have been noted in Islamic propaganda in recent years. In addition to extolling the religion of Islam, contemporary Muslim propaganda, both domestic and foreign, also devotes a great deal of attention to social morality, especially in conjunction with questions of the legalization of unsanctioned clerical activity and of pro-Islamic propaganda within the USSR.

For example, "national" religious songs are played widely, warning that the torments of hell wait "in the other world" for those who do not respect their parents (meaning the Islam of their parents). Such tapes can be bought freely in the bazaar in Kokand, and it is worth noting that these tapes are of professional quality, recorded in a sound studio. The clergy approve of and encourage listening to such music, as does public opinion. This is "national" music.

I have not known parents to object to their sons viewing video cassettes of pornographic films, which are illegally brought to the kishlaks by traveling entrepreneurs, who get fifty rubles for admission to a single show. Such "entertainment" does not contradict Islam, or at least I know of one unofficial mullah who did not condemn such "cultural activities," but instead gave his son the necessary sum without comment. An attempt by the organs of public order to prevent the showing of such films in that case was met by a wall of silence from the residents of the whole, very large kishlak, who defended the traveling video owners.

At the same time, this mullah and father forbade his son to have anything to do with members of our expedition, since we were "kafirs." Similarly, the teachers who actively assisted our expedition were ostracized by the community, after a trial organized by the village elders, the *aksakals*.

Special attention needs to be drawn to how little the great majority of the Central Asian people know about their own national cultures. Only a few people know the works of the great poets of the Middle Ages, like the Turkmen poet Makhtumkuli, or the Persian (Tajik) poets Jami, and Rudaki. In rural areas people know very little about their contemporary national classics and "Muslim" or Central Asian literature in general. When they finish middle school the majority of young people have absolutely no knowledge even of the modern professional cultural achievements of the Central Asian peoples who are their neighbors, let alone awareness of the achievements of world culture. The main cause of this is that they know Russian poorly or not at all, since Russian translates and transmits cultural attainments.

The degeneration of real national cultural values, in morals, ethics, artistic culture, folk art, song, and poetry is alarming, and it is quite clear that whole groups of artistic folk crafts have been lost. However, none of these phenomena concern the people who agitate for "national culture" in this particular Islamic form. If they touch upon the loss or disappearance of such spiritual and material values at all, it is only to claim it was caused by "the coming of the Russians."

Reactionary circles abroad are among the most passionate defenders of "national culture" in its Islamic interpretation. The world has recently become aware of this strategic alliance between the most reactionary part of the clergy and the military establishment, in the Irangate affair. However, these forces long ago united on the issue of anticommunism. Viewing traditionalism as the main anti-Soviet force in Central Asia, these reactionary circles have done all they can to parry criticism of traditionalism by characterizing its attributes as "national traditions," "national customs," and so forth.

The periodic campaigns in both East and West to "defend" Soviet Muslims always include representatives of the most reactionary circles, although we must also acknowledge that part of the fault lies with the feebleness of our own counterpropaganda. Foreign studies of the Basmachi are particularly poorly rebutted, since the tenacity with which many of our scholars cling to outmoded concepts and methods of historical study permits the foreign Islamicists to emerge from this debate victorious. Such was the case with the book *Basmachism: The Truth of History and the Invention of Falsifiers* [Basmachestvo: pravda istorii i vymysel fal'sifikatorov], by A.I. Zevelev, Iu.A. Poliakov, and

L.V. Shishkina, which probably did more harm than good because the authors' arguments were so painfully unconvincing, relying far more on rhetoric than upon analysis of factual data.

It is also a pity that our publications present traditionalism and everything associated with it as nothing more than harmless holdovers from the past that do not seriously affect the development of our society. Great pains are taken to avoid the study of the economic, social, and political structure of modern Central Asian society, even at the Institute of Oriental Studies of the Academy of Sciences of the USSR, which remains silent.*

Equally regrettable is that so many party workers, state officials, and senior scholars accept the Islamic interpretation of national culture. Whatever its cause, failure to understand the role traditionalism is playing in increasing social tension in Central Asia itself contributes to the further increase of tension in our country. At the moment this tension is the most negative aspect of traditionalism, requiring a more detailed examination. Although this will entail a certain repetition of material, I believe that will help make my argument clearer. I will base my argument upon Leninabad Oblast of the Tajik SSR because my most recent material is drawn from northern Tajikistan, and this area exhibits all the climatic zones and most of the types of economic activity that occur in Central Asia. In other words, this is a typical Central Asian region, where we may examine social tension and understand its historical causes.

---

*In the wake of the public disturbances in Central Asia in 1989 and 1990, several Soviet research institutions, including the Institute of Oriental Studies, have begun studying Central Asian Islam.

17

Social Tensions

> *Whatever evil happens to thee, is from thy own soul.*
> The Koran, IV, 79
>
> *Let not their speech grieve you!* The Koran, X, 65

In 1870, when Central Asia was joined to Russia, irrigated land and cattle—the economic basis of the people's existence—existed in sufficient amounts to sustain the average family in a state of semistarvation. By 1920 a family of five got a weekly supply of 3.5–4 kilos of grain (eight small flat breads), or 0.1–0.12 kg per person per day.[20] The meat supply was such that a family could slaughter no more than one ram a year (for a maximum of 40 kg of meat), meaning that in a year the average person got about 8 kg of meat. There was, of course, differentiation of class and property ownership; but even with fairly significant disparities in the amount of land available and, especially, the number of livestock owned, social and class oppression at the level of the kishlak was not as pronounced as it was in European Russia, both because of the peculiarities of Central Asian society and because important tribal and clan relations were preserved.

However, over the last third of the nineteenth century and the first third of the twentieth century, most of the population suffered a noticeable loss of land, with consequent impoverishment, and class differentiation and social and class oppression increased. The causes of this were both internal and external. Among the external causes were stabilization of the political situation in Central Asia after its union with Russia and the ending of civil strife. In addition, the contradictory policies of the Russian colonial administration also contributed. The primary task of these policies was to sever tribal and clan relationships among the animal-herding portion of the population both by administrative means (such as mixing herders of different tribes into administrative units instead of following tribal and clan divisions) and by economic ones (isolating them from grazing lands and to some degree from irrigated land).

Another factor was a policy that was basically progressive but was implemented without any regard for social and demographic processes. This policy regulated livestock herding in the mountains, with the intention of controlling grazing on sparse mountain vegetation (to preserve the ecological balance) and of encouraging a certain species definition of the herd (camels and goats were banned from grazing in the mountains, because they eat shrubs). Objectively these measures restricted the most profitable segment of the economy.

One result of political stability was a demographic "explosion," or significant growth in the population. As has been noted, between 1870 and 1931 the population in what today is Leninabad Oblast grew three and a half times. By the turn of the century the need to supply the growing population with food had already caused a noticeable increase in the amount of land being sown with grain. For all practical purposes, however, this growth came only from dry-land farming (which relied solely on rain). The growth possibilities of irrigated lands, given the level of the work force then, had been essentially exhausted by 1870, which made it impossible to produce necessary supplies let alone a surplus.

The result of these processes was social and psychological distress brought about by the sharp deterioration in the standard of living. The people, especially that part of the population in particular need, began to seek causes for this deterioration, which they found, with help from some of the traditionalists, in the presence of a Russian population in Central Asia.

The social expression of this tension was the broad formation and spread of the Basmachi, although the immediate stimulus for their appearance was the Russian government's move in 1916 to draft the local population for work behind the lines. Also important were the terrible famine of 1917–18, the events surrounding the establishment of Soviet rule, and the military destruction of the Khiva khanate and the emirate of Bukhara.

The creation of national boundaries in 1924, the land and water reforms of 1921–29, and the subsequent formation of collective farms lessened social tension in Central Asia for a time, but did nothing to remove the causes of tension and in some instances even created the conditions for making it worse in the future. (I have in mind the way in which the land and water reforms were introduced in some regions, returning cultivated steppe lands to pasturage, which made the grain shortage worse when cotton was subsequently introduced.)

The strength of "tribal and clan survivals" and the economic relations that accompany them meant that the first collective farms were created out of collectives of relatives, or avlods (in Tajikistan), in which the head of the extended family became the president of the collective farm. Such clans saw the collective farm land as the property of the avlod, and understood what the collective farm had to contribute to the state to be a natural tax for the land, as traditional practices sanction. (The allotment of land to the collective farms was naturally understood by the population to be a redistribution of the avlod land, which the majority of farmers were extremely reluctant to undertake.)

As the collective farms grew stronger they began to make up their work brigades and cells out of family and kinship groups; a similar principle was preserved, in a discreet way, on state farms as well.

In the 1960s, just as contradictions in the social and economic processes of the USSR as a whole began to grow, so did the hidden contradictions in Central Asian society begin to become more apparent, against a background of uncontrolled local population growth. Compared with 1870, and including immigration, the population of Leninabad Oblast was 10.5 times greater. Another factor intensifying these contradictions was the premature dissolution of collective farms and creation of state farms, which freed a significant portion of the working population from public production. Having minimal potential for outmigration, these workers directed all their physical and mental resources to gaining untaxed income. They were encouraged in this by the leveling of wages in the state farms, which were kept too low to support families of ten or more. In such conditions the entire rural population (and a good bit of the urban population as well) concentrated on making money from the personal use plots (of up to 0.15 hectares) and from privately established plots and pasturage in the mountains.

The ideological basis of this socially determined mass behavior and mass psychology was traditionalism, as represented by the "everyday" social institutions of the kishlak, the neighborhood, and the family, which were preserved at the lower levels of the state structure (with a significant measure of "tribal" survivals). The result was an increase in alternative petty commodity production, based on private agriculture. This type of production relies upon monocultural specialization by microregion and on uniform, specialized herds, and it possesses its own supporting alternative ideology.

On the ideological level this led to a sharp growth in nationalism, expressed in an open form among the rural population. Among the intelligentsia, this took a "scholarly" form; they praised everything that predated the Russians, and saw the past as a "golden age." This change also led to the growth of Muslim (or Islamic) ideology in national and traditionalist disguise, and to the strengthening of the traditional system of education that produces this ideology. On the demographic level the changes led to a significant number of the working population being removed from the public economy and engaging instead in the acquisition of very large untaxed incomes.

On the ecological level this led to mass destruction of land because of the uncontrolled application of chemical, nitrogen, and phosphate fertilizers (with the intention of stimulating early and very large harvests) as well as to cultivation of nonfood crops. Also to be considered is the massive destruction of pasturage caused by grazing uncontrolled numbers of unvariegated herds in the mountains. The result is the loss of mountain juniper cover over large areas and the consequent denuding of the mountains, which has negative environmental consequences. The natural mountain water-drainage system has been destroyed and water supplies for a whole number of regions have been squandered. This has led to changes in the mountain grass cover, a drop in dry-land farming, widespread scree washouts, and depletion of the land reserves, as good arable land plots are transformed into sterile desert where no plants grow.

On the financial level these changes have meant the removal from circulation in the state economy of significant amounts of money, which the population ties up in commodities. This is possible because of the persistence of traditional ways of life and the consequent refusal to spend money on socially enlightened, positive expenses.

On the societal level the consequence has been the regeneration, in exaggerated form, of customs and traditions that had different economic and sociodemographic bases in the past and in present conditions only strengthen negative social and economic processes. As a whole, all this has strengthened the mechanisms that preserve the "outmoded" features of oriental society and retard its social development, threatening the realization of Soviet society's goals for development.

We may conclude from this that traditionalism in Central Asia has grown too much to be considered a "survival," for it now behaves as a system that is opposed to our order. The absolute majority of the Central Asian people consider themselves Muslim. This is manifested not just in a religious world view but in the entire way of life, which is based on a petty commodity economy that in places has grown into private enterprise. V.I. Lenin characterized the political significance of this way of life in a whole range of his works.

Today in Central Asia there are two levels in ideology, just as there are two levels in the economy. The first is the state level, adequate for addressing the state sector on all-union issues; the second is the "family" level, based on petty commodity production. On the "everyday" level too, there is a double perception of the real way of life. The "state" evaluation of tradition is that it is bad; the "family" view is that it is good, the proper way of life. Here we again encounter the unprincipled nature of traditionalism, mentioned above.

It follows that analysis of the function of traditionalism must be radically restructured, because the peaceful stage of traditionalism's development has ended. Traditionalists can only interpret our inactivity in this regard to mean the weakness of Soviet rule. The legalization of all the activities of traditionalist institutions, such as mazars and underground maktabs, is a reality. Increasingly traditionalism is demanding the status of a system beyond state control, one that takes no account of society's needs. Also dangerous is the fact that many party members are infected by traditionalist ideology. Extremism is acquiring dangerous dimensions. The doctor and writer Fazliddin Mukhamadiev, author of the progressive book *Journey to the Other World* [Puteshestvie na tot svet], was brutally murdered, and the editor of *Komsomolets Tadzhikistana* died under mysterious circumstances. A female instructor of the Chardui Oblast party committee (Turkmenistan) was viciously strangled. Central Asian society is waiting for the hour when "the traditionalists of Central Asia will throw off Moscow's oppression." All of this is real, and cannot be ignored. This struggle between two ideologies will be intense and long, because there are an enormous number of people among us already who have been educated in a traditional way.

However, these people—young, middle-aged, and old—are all citizens of the Soviet Union. Though the family petty commodity economy dictates the conditions of life, far from all of them live by such methods. Central Asian society, like any other society, consists of various social groups and levels, who do not take identical positions with regard to traditionalism. In fact, rooting out those factors that keep the traditional system alive in our society must be undertaken *only* after careful advance study of and consideration for these various positions. It must be accepted as a given that traditionalism in Central Asia is an objective reality, like it or not. Such objectivity is based on the economic structure of rural Central Asian society, as explained in this book; it follows that battling the influence of traditionalism using only ideological methods is unrealistic. If we fail to understand this, then we also fail to understand the essence of traditionalism.

NOTES

1. See N.Kh. Azimova, *Sistema peredachi informatsii detiam v uzbekskikh sem'iakh*, manuscript, archive of the Ethnography Department, Moscow State University, 1986; B.B. Akmoldoeva, *Konevodstvo v sisteme traditsionnogo khoziaistva kirgizov (konets XIX–nachalo XX vv.)*, dissertation for the degree of *kandidat istoricheskikh nauk*, 1983; M. Faizullaev, *Tadzhiki predgorii severnogo Tadzhikistana. Khoziaistvo i sotsial'naia organizatsiia (konets XIX–pervaia tret' XX vv.)*, dissertation for the degree of *kandidat istoricheskikh nauk*, 1987; V.I. Bushkov, Naselenie severnogo Tadzhikistana (formirovanie i rasselenie), dissertation for the degree of *kandidat istoricheskikh nauk*, 1988; idem, *Sel'skie mecheti severnogo Tadzhikistana*, manuscript, archive of the Ethnography Department, Moscow State University, 1988; S.P. Poliakov, *Metodika izucheniia pogrebal'nykh sooruzhenii (Srednıaıa Aziia X—XX vv.)*, INION AN SSSR, 1988, n. 36106.
2. V.I. Lenin, *Polnoe sobranie sochinenii*, vol. 14, p. 120.
3. S.P. Poliakov, *Istoricheskaia etnografiia Srednei Azii i Kazakhstana* (Moscow: Moscow State Univerity, 1980), pp. 23–81.
4. V.V. Barthold, *Sochineniia*, vol. VI (Moscow: Nauka, 1966).
5. K. Marx, *Ekonomicheskie rukopisi 1857–1861 gg. (Pervonachal'nyi variant "Kapitala")*, Part I (Moscow, 1980), p. 469.
6. Poliakov, *Istoricheskaia etnografiia*, pp. 107ff.
7. For details see ibid., p. 81.
8. K. Marx and F. Engels, *Sochineniia*, vol. 9.
9. See M.T. Stepaniants, *Musul'manskie kontseptsii v filosofii i politike (XIX—XX vv)*, Moscow, 1982.
10. "The *petite bourgeoisie* is the class of urban and rural small private-holders who live exclusively or primarily on the fruits of their own labor." *Sovetskii entsiklopedicheskii slovar'* (Moscow, 1980), p. 796.
11. *Vosstanie 1916 g. v Srednei Azii i Kazakhstane. Sbornik dokumentov* (Moscow: Izdatel'stvo AN SSR, 1960), pp. 15–21. This revolt was centered in Kyrgyzstan and southern Kazakhstan; there was less resistance in some Uzbek areas.
12. Marx, and Engels, *Sochineniia*, vol. 19, p. 208.
13. Lenin, *Polnoe sobranie sochinenii*, vol. 3.

14. Ibid., vol. 2, p. 285.
15. Ibid., vol. 1, pp. 71–122.
16. V.I. Bushkov, "Naselenie Khodzhenta i ego okrugi," in *Issledovaniia po istorii i kul'ture Leninabada* (Dushanbe: Donish, 1986), p. 175.
17. In 1986 Central Asian authorities limited the use of college and secondary-school students in the cotton harvest, but to little effect.
18. See N.A. Kisliakov, *Ocherki po istorii sem'i i braka u narodov Srednei Azii i Kazakhstana* (Leningrad, 1969), and idem, *Nasledovanie i razdel imushchestva u narodov Srednei Azii i Kazakhstana* (Leningrad, 1977) (both with bibliography).
19.. V.V. Mavrodin, ed., *Istoriia SSSR: Chast' pervaia: S drevneishikh vremen do 1861 g.* 4th ed., expanded and corrected (Moscow: "Prosveshchenie," 1979).
20. Faizullaev, *Tadzhiki predgorii Severnogo Tadzhikistana.*

Index of Subjects

Adat (customary law), 17, 29, 78
Agriculture, 24, 39, 43–44
   child labor, 59, 60–61, 123–24
   climate conditions, 24
   collective farms, 14 (Table 2), 17, 23, 28, 30, 103, 140–41
   crops, 24–25
   family labor, 27
   farm machinery, 27
   government transport, use of, 27
   industrialization in, 115–16
   irrigation system. *See* Irrigation systems.
   land-plots. *See* Land-plots.
   narcotic substances grown, 25
   public versus private interests, 117
   seasonal workers, 119
   state farms, 14 (Table 2), 23, 28, 30, 43, 44, 141
Angora goats, breeding of, 26, 48
Apricot orchards, 30, 34, 63, 116
Arabic language, 74, 110, 133
"Asiatic feudalism," 11, 12
Avlod (clan), 15, 17, 76, 100, 140

Barthold, V.V., 10
Basmachi movement, 18–19, 100n, 136–37, 140
Bibiotun (female religious figure), 72, 73 (Table 7), 78, 89
   pro-Islamic agitation by, 112
   role of, 74, 109–10
   training for, 110
Birth rate, 56

Black market, 46
Bribery
   amount of bribes, 47
   attempts to end, 47
   crop prices, 117n
   land-plots, acquisition through, 29, 49
   "legality," 91
   police activities, 49
   prevalence of, 46–47
   public opinion, 47, 49

Caliphs, 100n, 133
Capitalism, 13, 15
Carrot crops, 30
Cemeteries. *See* Graveyards.
Central Asia
   areas included in study of, 6
   ethnic representation, 8 (Table 1)
Central Asian Expedition of the History Faculty of Moscow State University
   areas studied, 6
   research methodology, 7–8
Child labor, 59, 60–61, 123–24
"Child's cycle" rituals, 90
Circumcision celebration, 56, 57, 89
Civil construction
   training schools (PTUs), 120
   workers for, 120–21
Collectivization, 12, 17, 19
Colonialism. *See* Russian colonial administration.

148 INDEX

Communist party, 72, 118–19, 121, 137. *See also* Komsomol.
Construction. *See* Civil construction.
Cooperatives, 35
Cotton production, 39, 44
  child labor, 61
  Uzbekistan cotton sandals, 23*n*

Dervish orders, descendants of, 107–8
Divorce, 58, 85
  infertility as cause of, 62
  protest against planned marriage, 65
  women and, 62–63, 65–66, 85
Dowry, 57. *See also* Marriage.

Economic structure
  agriculture. *See* Agriculture.
  distribution of income, 35–37 (Tables 4, 5), 88, 103, 116–17
  family economy. *See* Family economy.
  generally, 9, 23, 116
  land-plots. *See* Land-plots.
  livestock production. *See* Livestock production.
  petty commodity. *See* Petty commodity economy.
  private-sector. *See* Private-sector economy.
  state sector. *See* State-sector economy.
Education
  Arabic language, instruction in, 74, 110, 153
  Arab literature, 133
  elementary, 123–24
  employment preparation, for, 115, 130
  higher, 124–25, 130
  history, 126–28
  humanities, 125–26
  industrial training, 115
  information sources, 73 (Table 7), 74
  marriage costs to family, effect of, 57

Education *(continued)*
  nationalism and, 125–28
  national culture, 133–34, 135–36
  religious. *See* Religious education.
  Russian language, instruction in, 115, 129, 133, 136
  social sciences, 125–26
  specialists, 124–25
  technical professions, 129
  traditionalism and, 126
  women's role in children's, 66–67
Elders, 92, 97
Employment, 39, 43–44, 116
Ethnic representation, 8 (Table 1)

Family budget
  "child's cycle" rituals, cost of, 90
  circumcision celebration costs, 89
  family income production and, 45
  funeral costs, 89–90
  Islamic holidays, cost of, 90
  "nonrational" expenditures, 87, 88 (Figure 3)
  "rational" expenditures, 87, 88 (Figure 3), 89
  research on, 87
  wedding costs, 89
Family economy
  expenses and taxes, 28
  family budget. *See* Family budget.
  family income production, 45
  income not subject to taxes, 29
  land-plots, 28, 29
  political structure, 138–39
  religious rituals. *See* Religious rituals.
  state sector of, 27–28
  See also Petty commodity economy.
Family structure
  boy's role in, 60, 80
  economic structure and, 138–39
  forty-year-old men, 58, 67, 82–83
  girl's role, 59–60, 66, 80
  grandfather's role in, 82–83
  husband's role as provider, 84

Family structure *(continued)*
  kelin (young wife), 66
  Married son, status of, 58
  mother-in-law (husband's mother), 66, 80
  preschool children, 80
  separation of married son from family, 58, 67, 82–83
  size of family, 45
  teenage girls, 66
  undivided family, 58
  women's position in, 84
  young men and women, 80, 81–82
  "youth problems," 91
Farms. *See* Collective farms, State farms.
Folk healers, 62
Funeral costs, 89–90

Genghis Khan, 130, 132
Graveyards, 16, 98, 99–100, 101, 102, 109

Haji (pilgrims), 101, 107, 108, 130
Health, 59, 101
History, study of, 126–28
Housing shortages, 121, 122
Hujra (religious structures), 97
Humanities, study of, 125–26

Illegal trade, 34, 38
Imam (prayer leader), 14, 80, 105, 140
  election of, 109
Industrial skills, acquisition of, 115, 119
Industrial workers, 116, 117
  housing, 121–22
  " 'imported," 120
  outmigration of Europeans, 122
  qualified workers, 120–21
  training, 115, 119
Industrialization
  agriculture, 115–16
  family ties and, 117
  mining, 117–18

Industrialization *(continued)*
  traditionalism, effect of, 117–18
  women and, 117
Infant-mortality rates, 40, 56–57
Infertility, 61, 62, 100
Institute of Oriental Studies, 137
Institute of Scientific Atheism, 134
Intelligentsia, 123, 125
  technical specialties, 129–30
  traditionalism and "national" culture, 130–37
  training, 124–28
Interethnic relations, 33, 120
Irangate affair, 136
Irrigation systems
  family economic structure and, 27
  mahalla control of, 77
  social structure and, 12–13
  Soviet control of, 16, 139
Islam
  adaptability of, 16
  Arab conquest, 132–33
  historical background, 15, 131–33
  "Islamic culture," 131–32, 133–34, 136
  Islamic law (shari'a), 12, 17, 29, 38, 41, 42, 47, 64, 71, 78, 82, 85
  preservation of, 107
  propaganda, 111–12, 135
  See also Traditionalism.

Jami, 135
Jungid Khan, 18

Kalym (bride-price), 54–58, 60
Karakum-ishan, 18
Khamza, 132
Khan, 14, 16–17, 107, 130, 132
Kolkhoz. *See* Collective farms.
Komsomol, 79, 119
Koran
  regulation of life by, 12, 15, 16
  religious and social structure, 12
  Soviet rule and, 16–17
  text of instruction, 74
Wahhabism, 4

Land-plots
  allowable plot size per family, 29
  bribery, use in acquiring, 29, 49
  categories of, 28
  environmental destruction of, 30, 42, 45
  forms of ownership, 14 (Table 2)
  illegalities in allotments, 29, 30–31
  livestock, for, 49
  private-plot production, 24–26 (Table 3)
  "reclaimed," 29
Livestock production
  distribution of income, 35
  environmental destruction, 48
  excessive herds, 48–49
  land-plots for, trade in, 49
  meat prices, 49
  overgrazing, 48
  private control of, 47–48
  record-keeping, 49, 50
  uniform versus varied herds, 48

Magi, 132
Mahalla (neighborhood)
  avlod transformed into, 76
  committees of. *See* Neighborhood committees.
  information of transmission within, 79
  power of, 78–79
  rebellious behavior, sanctions for, 78
  religious education, role in, 75, 79
  Soviet recognition of, 77
  Soviet rule, effect of, 76–77
  women and, 78
Maktab (underground religious school), 14, 67, 73 (Table 7), 74, 105, 143
Manual labor, extent of, 39
Marriage
  bride, selection of, 53–54
  costs, effect on family, 57
  dowry, 57
  girls' attitudes toward, 83–84

Marriage *(continued)*
  husband's role as provider, 84
  kalym (bride-price), 54–58, 60
  marriageable age, 71
  married women, standards of behavior, 83
  modern bride *(ill.)*, 65
  mother-in-law (husband's mother), role of, 53–54
  multiple wives, 62–63, 85
  obligatory, 41
  planned event, 53–54
  registration of, 63, 64, 84–85
  relations between spouses, 84
  traditional bride *(ill.)*, 64
  wedding costs, 57, 89
  women's protests against, 85–86
Marx, Karl, 23
Mazar (holy shrine), 72, 73, 99
  budget, 102–3
  infertility, treatment of, 100
  legalization of functions of, 109
  maintenance and repair of, 101, 102
  mosque, merger with, 108–9
  mosque, mazars functioning as, 102
  "power" of, 100–101
  sanctity, 100, 108
  screens hiding, 103–4
  services and prayers, 109
  sheik of. *See* Sheik.
  strength within society, 108
Meat prices, 49
Medresseh (seminary), 95, 105
Men
  behavior, 44, 81–82
  boys, role in society, 60
  divorce and, 58–85
  forty-year-olds, 58, 67, 82–83
  grandfathers, role of, 67–69
  opportunities, 115–16
  provider, role as, 84
  second wives, 62–63
Meskhetian Turks, 81
Mining, 117–18

Mosque
  activities within, 98–99
  budget, 102–3
  construction and maintenance of, 96
  eating-places, 98–99
  holiness, as symbol of, 98
  nonfunctioning, 97–98
  numbers, 95n, 96
  official mosques, 95
  religious training, 72, 73 (Table 3), 79–80
  sanctity, 98, 108
  screens hiding, 103–4
  state-approved, 106–7
  underground mosques, 96
  unofficial mosques, 106–7
Mountain areas
  condition of, 42
Muhammad, 69, 100, 107
Mukhamadiev, Fazliddin, 143
Mullah (cleric)
  official, 105, 106, 107n
  privileges of, 110–11
  regional divisions, 108
  traditional clerical families, 107, 110–11
  unofficial, 105–7, 109, 110–11
Muslim Spiritual Administration of Central Asia and Kazakhstan (SADUM), 105n

Nakhshaban, Bakh ad-din, 107
Narcotic crops, 25
Nationalism, 125, 128, 141
Neighborhood committees, 77–78
  control and influence of, 111–12
  election of members, 111
  payment of members, 111

Otynch. *See* Bibiotun.
Outmigration (Europeans), 122
Overpopulation, 41, 44, 115, 139
  standard of living and, 139–40

Pasha, Enver, 100n

Petty commodity economy
  adults working in, 32, 43, 143
  agriculture, 24–26 (Table 3)
  defined, 26
  environment, effect on, 30
  family structure and, 53, 58
  illegal income, necessity for, 38
  "industrial buyer," 32–33
  interethnic relations, effect on, 33
  livestock production, 26
  middlemen, 33–34, 35, 37 (Table 5)
  price-setting, 34
  rackets and racketeering, presence of, 35, 37
  regulation of, 34
  "rural seller," 32–33
  shortages, artificial, 34
  state losses attributable to, 33
  state sector, relation to, 26–28
  transport of freight, 35, 37
  undivided families and, 58
  working class and, 119
Population
  annexation to Russia, effect of, 40
  birth rate, 56
  increases, 40–41, 56–57
  infant-mortality rates, 40, 56–57
  overpopulation, 41, 44, 115, 139–40
Potato crop, 30
Price-setting of goods, 34
Private-sector economy
  generally, 24–26 (Table 3)
  distribution of income, 35–37 (Tables 4, 5)
  family size, effect on, 45
  government studies of, 26
  See also Petty commodity economy.
PTUs (technical training schools), 120

Ramadan, 90
Rebellious behavior
  social sanctions for, 90–91
Religious education
  bibiotun, role of, 72, 73, 74, 78, 86

Religious education *(continued)*
  boys, 70 (Table 6), 71, 72, 73 (Table 7), 79, 92
  elders, 91–92
  girls, 70 (Table 6), 71, 72, 73 (Table 7), 79–80, 86, 92
  grandfather's role in, 69
  mahalla, role in, 75, 79, 86
  mazar, role of, 72
  mosques, importance of, 72, 79, 86
  preschoolers, 67, 72, 80, 86
  sources of information, 72, 73 (Table 7), 74–75, 86
  submission, as system of, 91
  transmission of information, 67
  women's role in, 66–67, 112
Religious institutions
  numbers of, 95*n*, 96
  See also specific headings
Religious rituals
  costs, 38, 56, 57, 59, 88–90
  exclusion from, 78
  petty commodity economy and, 38
  See also specific headings
Riba (usurious interest), 103
Rudaki, 3, 135
Russian colonial administration, 13, 15, 18, 40, 126, 139
Russian language skills, 115, 129, 133, 136

SADUM (Muslim Spiritual Administration of Central Asia and Kazakhstan), 105*n*
Samarkand, 6, 8, 108
Seasonal workers, 119
Seid (descendant of Muhammad), 107, 118
Shari'a (Islamic law), 12, 17, 38, 41, 42, 47, 64, 71, 78, 82, 85
Sheik (mazar guardian), 101–2, 107
  influence of, 108
  position, battle for, 109
  Soviet authorities and, 109
  women and, 108
Shi'ism, 100, 134
Shortages, 34
Social mobility, 115
Social position
  financial status and, 124
Social stratification, 10
Social sciences, study of, 125–26
Social tensions
  Basmachi movement, 18–19, 100*n*, 136–37, 140
  economic basis of, 138–39
  overpopulation, 139
Soviet Army, 119
Soviet government
  attitudes toward, 18–19, 29, 38, 40, 49, 100, 143
  irrigation systems, control of, 16, 139
  land ownership under, 14 (Table 2), 16–17
  traditionalism, control of, 142–44
Soviet law
  disrespect for, 82
  Shari'a, comparison to, 29, 82
State farms, 14 (Table 2), 23, 28, 30, 43, 44, 141
State-sector economy, 23–24
  employment within, 41–42, 44
  salaries, 38
Sufism, 97, 107
Sunnat-toi (circumcision celebration), 56, 57, 89
Sunnism, 134

Timur (Tamerlane), 132
Tobacco farming, 25, 61
Toi. *See* Religious rituals.
Traditionalism
  anti-Sovietism and, 19
  defined, 4
  growth of, 8–9
  ideological superstructure, 4
  industrial settlements, in, 117
  mining settlements, in, 117–18
  oil worker families and, 118
  preservation of, 133–34

Traditionalism *(continued)*
  religious authority versus civil authority, 12
  Soviet attitudes toward, 19, 137
  study of, 8–10, 12
  transmission of information under, 4
  See also specific headings.
Transport of goods, 27
Tura (descendants of Genghis Khan), 107, 130

Ulema, 5, 11
Unemployment, 116
Uprising of 1916, 18

Wahhabism, 4
Waqf lands, 14 (Table 2), 103
Weddings
  cost of, 57, 89
  modern bride (*ill.*), 65
  traditional bride (*ill.*), 64
  See also Marriage.
Women
  bibiotun, role amongst, 72, 74, 78, 109–10
  divorce, 62–63, 65–66
  education of children, role in, 66–67
  employment, 42–43, 44, 117
  family structure and, 83
  farm laborers, 61

Women *(continued)*
  financial independence and, 83
  girls, socialization of, 83–84
  industrial workers, as, 117
  industrialized villages, in, 64–65
  infertility, 61, 62
  kelin (young wife), 66
  mahalla committees and, 77
  marriageable age, 71
  married women, standards of behavior, 83
  mosques and, 79–80
  public production, exclusion from, 42
  rural women, 63
  Sheiks, influence of, 108
  social status of, 63
  suicide as protest against marriage, 85–86
  women's councils, 79
  See also specific headings.
Women's councils, 79
Working class, 115, 117
  housing, 121–22
  interethnic relations, 120
  petty commodity economy and, 119
  seasonal workers, 119
  societal development and, 119–20
  traditionalism and, 119–20

Zevelev, A.I., 136
Zoroastrianism, 8, 98

Index of Place Names

Akhal oasis, 119
Alma-Ata (capital, Kazakhstan), 9, 81, 132
Andijan Oblast (Uzbekistan), 44, 56–57, 65, 120, 133
Angren (Uzbekistan), 64
Armenia, 81
Ashkhabad (capital, Turkmenistan), 118–119
Asht Raion (Tajikistan), 19, 28, 34, 56–57, 63, 86
Avchi (village, Ganchin Raion, Tajikistan), 17

Baku (capital, Azerbaizan), 81
Balkhash, Lake, 6
Bishkek. *See* Frunze.
Bukhara, 6, 18, 95, 100, 105, 140

Caucausus, 17
Chadak (village, Namangan Oblast, Uzbekistan), 101
Chardui Oblast (Turkmenistan), 143
Chorku (village, Leninabad Oblast, Tajikistan), 34

Dnieper Basin, 128
Dushanbe (Tajikistan), 95, 98, 118, 121

Fergana valley, 6, 8, 41, 44, 63, 77, 81, 96, 108, 111
Frunze (capital, Kyrgyzstan), 121

Ganchin Raion, 17, 30, 42, 48–49, 109, 115, 124

Hojant. *See* Khodzhent; *See also* Leninabad.

Iran, 134
Isfara Raion (Tajikistan), 34, 44, 63, 96, 117

Karl Marx State Farm, 42, 44, 48
Kashkadaria Oblast, 6
Kazakhstan, 6, 81, 132
Khivan Khanate, 13, 140
Khodzhent, 128
Khorezm, 8, 108
KIM (town, Isfara Raion, Tajikistan), 65, 117
Kirgizia, 6, 18, 34, 47, 89, 101, 122. *See also* Osh Oblast.
Kokand Khanate, 13, 96
Kuchkak (village, Isfara Raion, Tajikistan), 65, 117
Kyrgyzstan. *See* Kirgizia.
Kyzylarvat Raion (Turkmenistan), 101

Leninabad Oblast (Tajikistan), 8, 17, 19, 34, 40–42, 48–49, 63, 86, 98, 106, 117–118, 120, 124, 139–140. *See also* Asht Raion; Ganchin Raion.
Leningrad, 128

154

INDEX   155

Mangyshlak Oblast (Kazakhstan), 6, 9, 108
Mecca, 16, 109
Metk (village, Ganchin Raion, Tajikistan), 30, 109, 115, 124
Moscow, 34, 82, 118, 124, 128, 143

Namangam Oblast (Uzbekistan), 78, 101
Nefteabad (village, Tajikistan), 118

Osh Oblast (Kyrgyzstan), 43, 47, 89, 101

Pangaz (village, Asht Raion, Tajikistan), 44, 63–65, 97
Paraubibi (mazar), 101

Regarskii Metallurgical Complex, 120
Rosrovut (village, Ganchin Raion, Tajikistan), 30
Russia, 126, 139

Samarkand Oblast (Uzbekistan), 6, 8, 108
Shurabe (village, Isfara Raion, Tajikistan), 118

Suleiman's Mountain (mazar), 101
Sumgait, 81

Tajikistan, 5, 6, 18, 28–30, 34, 41–42, 48, 57, 63, 72, 76, 96, 98–100, 109, 115, 117, 119, 120, 121, 133, 140, 143. *See also* Leninabad Oblast.
Tashkent (capital, Uzbekistan), 95
Turkestan, 18, 43, 100
Turkmenistan, 6, 18–19, 55, 99–101, 118–119, 134. *See also* Chardui Oblast; Kyzylarvat Oblast.
Turkey, 100

Unji (village, Leninabad Oblast, Tajikistan), 98
Ura-tiube (city, Tajikistan), 119
Uzbekistan, 8, 18, 23, 42, 44, 54, 56, 65, 81, 101, 111, 120, 122, 132. *See also* Andijan Oblast; Kashkadaria Oblast; Namangan Oblast; Samarkand Oblast.

Varukh (village, Isfara Raion, Tajikistan), 44, 63, 96, 103, 106, 108
Zeravshan valley, 133

SERGEI P. POLIAKOV is an ethnographer who has for many years directed the Central Asian Expedition of the History Faculty of Moscow State University.

MARTHA B. OLCOTT, professor of political science at Colgate University, is a specialist on the former Soviet Union. She is the author of *The Kazakhs* as well as numerous articles on Soviet and post-Soviet politics.